THINKING ABOUT EDUCATION SERIES
FOURTH EDITION
Jonas F. Soltis, *Editor*

The revised and expanded Fourth Edition of this series builds on the strengths of the previous editions. Written in a clear and concise style, these books speak directly to preservice and in-service teachers. Each offers useful interpretive categories and thought-provoking insights into daily practice in schools. Numerous case studies provide a needed bridge between theory and practice. Basic philosophical perspectives on teaching, learning, curriculum, ethics, and the relation of school to society are made readily accessible to the reader.

PERSPECTIVES ON LEARNING
D. C. Phillips and Jonas F. Soltis

THE ETHICS OF TEACHING
Kenneth A. Strike and Jonas F. Soltis

CURRICULUM AND AIMS
Decker F. Walker and Jonas F. Soltis

SCHOOL AND SOCIETY
Walter Feinberg and Jonas F. Soltis

APPROACHES TO TEACHING
Gary D Fenstermacher and Jonas F. Soltis

FOURTH EDITION

APPROACHES
to TEACHING

GARY D FENSTERMACHER
University of Michigan

JONAS F. SOLTIS
Teachers College, Columbia University

Teachers College
Columbia University
New York and London

Published by Teachers College Press, 1234 Amsterdam Avenue, New York, NY 10027

Library of Congress Cataloging-in-Publication Data

Fenstermacher, Gary D
   Approaches to Teaching / Gary D Fenstermacher, Jonas F. Soltis.—4th ed.
     p. cm. — (Thinking about education series)
   Includes bibliographical references.
   ISBN 0-8077-4448-4
    1. Teaching. 2. Effective teaching. 3. Case method. 4. Education—Philosophy.
   I. Soltis, Jonas F. II. Title. III. Series
   LB1025.3.F46 2004
   371.102—dc 22   2004048068

ISBN 0-8077-4448-4 (paper)

Printed on acid-free paper
Manufactured in the United States of America

11 10 09 08 07 06 05 04   8 7 6 5 4 3 2 1

Contents

Acknowledgments   *ix*

A Note to Readers   *xi*

Chapter 1
APPROACHES TO TEACHING   1
    Three Teachers   1
    The Amazing Glasses   4
    Three Approaches to Teaching   5
    The Common Framework: MAKER   7
    Using MAKER with the Approaches   9

Chapter 2
THE EXECUTIVE APPROACH   11
    Managing Your Classroom   11
    Managing Time in the Classroom   12
    Features of This Approach   15
    The MAKER Framework   16
    Historical Roots   19
    Teaching for Student Achievement   21
    The Complexity of Modern Schooling   23

Chapter 3
THE FACILITATOR APPROACH   25
    Your Middle School English Class   26
    Historical Background   28
    Humanistic Psychology   30
    Normative Considerations   32
    Existential Roots   33
    Care Pedagogy   34
    Facilitating Identity   37
    Constructivism   39
    Multiple Intelligences   41

Chapter 4
THE LIBERATIONIST APPROACH   44
    Origins of This Approach   44
    Features of the Liberationist Approach   45
    Your High School Class   46
    Manner in Teaching   47
    The Element of Knowledge   49
    Emancipatory Teaching   51
    Democratic Citizenship   53
    Social Justice and Identity   55

Chapter 5
REFLECTIONS ON THE THREE APPROACHES   57
    A Synoptic View   57
    Critical Perspectives on the Executive Approach   59
    Critical Perspectives on the Facilitator Approach   61
    Forging National Identity   63
    Critical Perspectives on the Liberationist Approach 65
    Democracy, Identity, and Diversity   68

Chapter 6
DEVELOPING YOUR APPROACH TO TEACHING   71
    Three Ideas, Three Approaches   71
    Becoming All Three   73
    Good-bye   74

Chapter 7
CASES AND DISPUTES   76
    Grading Policies   78
    School and Approach Mismatch   79
    Teacher-Engineer or Artist?   80
    Individualized Learning   82
    How Much Control Is Too Much?   83
    Workbook Dilemma   83
    A New Science Kit   84
    Individual and Societal Needs   86
    Curing Shyness   86
    What Standard Shall We Use?   87
    Teaching "Relevant" Literature   89
    Teacher and Mother?   90
    Freedom and Indoctrination   90
    Too Young to Be Critical?   91

Education for Life   92
Freedom of Speech?   93
Mass or Class Culture?   95
Learning Chemistry by Discussion   96
Different Learning Styles   98
Compatibility of Approaches   98
E Pluribus Unum   99
Go Fly a Kite   100

Notes   *103*

Annotated Bibliography   *107*

Acknowledgments

We would like to thank a number of institutions and individuals that have contributed in different ways to the first writing of this book and to the completion of subsequent editions. They include, from Teachers College Press, Tom Rotell, Lois Patton, Carole Saltz, Sarah Biondello, Peter Sieger, Mel Berk, Nancy Power, Karl Nyberg, and our very helpful editor, Susan Liddicoat. Fran Simon provided word-processing skills for the first edition. Karl Hostetler served as research assistant and jack-of-all-trades for the first edition. He and the following people contributed ideas for the "Cases and Disputes" chapter: Tim Counihan, Susan Moyers, Barbara Reynolds, Janet Skupien, and Michael Weinstock. David Berliner and Lee Shulman shared their scholarship and friendship for the early editions. In the second edition, Susan Soltis gave us a perceptive description of the facilitator-teacher at work. Nancy Soltis, even with rapidly diminishing eyesight, continued as she had in earlier editions to efficiently support our fourth edition efforts with her computer skills and caring. Virginia Richardson, forgiving spouse of Gary and superb scholar in her own right, has been a critical friend, in the very best sense of the term, through all four editions of the book. Appreciation and thanks are due the University of Michigan's School of Education and its Dean, Karen Wixson, for a sabbatical leave that provided the time and energy required for this latest edition. Gary also extends his thanks to the Carnegie Foundation for the Advancement of Teaching and its President, Lee S. Shulman, for providing support while on leave during the 2003–04 academic year. Jonas and Gary would like to acknowledge each other's good colleagueship and friendship over the years and their shared love and concern for teaching. And last but not least, we thank our own teachers, students, and colleagues who have encouraged us to think deeply about teaching and prodded us to write these many editions.

A Note to Readers

We wrote this book using a style and tone that assumes it will be assigned early in an educational foundations or introduction to teaching course. No prior understanding of professional teaching literature is presumed, and the informality of style is deliberately intended to draw the reader into the material as quickly as possible. It is our hope that the book will engage the reader in both the practical and the theoretical aspects of teaching, while demonstrating how theory and practice are interdependent. Indeed, our desire to write this book was strongly motivated by the hope that we might show teacher candidates how theory and practice inform one another. We believe that it is one of the great misfortunes of modern schooling that its moment-to-moment demands on the teacher's attention are so enormous that many teachers cope by depreciating theory while depending too much on unreflected experience.

Extensive and considered use of the cases and disputes in chapter 7 is one of the best ways we know to demonstrate the interdependence of theory and practice. These cases and disputes are designed to bring the different approaches to teaching "alive," to show how the concepts and ideas that constitute the approaches bear on the actual practice of teaching and on situations that may arise in the course of teaching. We strongly recommend, therefore, that as each chapter is concluded, the cases and disputes relevant to that chapter be thoroughly explored (see table 2 in chapter 7 for a list of cases and disputes and the chapter numbers appropriate to them). Reminders to do so are frequent, and we hope the reader heeds them.

Lively and productive discussions of the cases and disputes are immeasurably aided by following these simple guidelines:

1. Good discussions require a climate of mutual respect. Participants should be free to express their views without fear of censure or ridicule, but should also be comfortable challenging one another with good evidence, reasonable argument, and alternative perspectives.
2. Good discussions depend on each participant's reading the case or dispute and formulating a tentative reaction prior to the initiation of group discussion.
3. Good discussions call for listening with the same care as is needed for talking. It is particularly beneficial when participants check their un-

derstanding of another participant's point before offering a reaction or critique.

4. Good discussions are helped when the instructor assists by summarizing views along the way, by making sure the key ideas are addressed, and by bringing about a measure of closure before moving on.

Such discussions can be successful in both whole-class and small-group formats, depending on the goals of the instructor and the needs of the students. We have enjoyed using some cases and disputes in both formats, beginning with small groups and moving to the whole class, as well as pursuing other cases and disputes only in small groups or with the entire class.

Just a few more brief items before you dig into the main text. First, we recommend that readers make extensive use of the World Wide Web for finding out more about what is contained in this book and for checking on how we may have interpreted what we are describing. Just open a search engine such as Google, Yahoo, or Ask Jeeves and type in the words you want to explore. For example, as you read in this book about constructivist teaching or multiple intelligences, you will be amazed (and informed) by what you find on the Web when you search these terms. Some words of caution, however: First, much of what you will turn up will be dated, so be sure to check on how current the information is. Second, the Web is an ideologue's delight, calling for a critical eye and a skeptical mindset. We encourage instructors to offer their students guidance on how to use the Web effectively so as to learn more about teaching, learning, and education in general.

We handle the gender reference of pronouns by simply alternating between *he* and *she*. Sometimes the teacher is male, and other times, female. Also, if we state the title of an article or book in the main text (rather than reserving the citation for the endnotes), we are suggesting that the reader will find the work accessible, interesting, and helpful. Works not mentioned in the main text that also meet these standards are noted in the Annotated Bibliography at the end of the book.

This book is designed to be used in a number of ways, depending on the purposes and teaching style of the instructor. It may be used as a primary text or as supplemental reading, or as a source book for cases and disputes that illuminate fundamental issues in education. We believe that this book can also be used effectively in staff development and in-service programs, providing experienced teachers with useful tools with which to examine and reflect on their practice. Any or all of the four other texts in this series can be used in conjunction with this book. They all have similar formats and styles.

Finally, to the students reading this book, we commend you for your interest in teaching and wish you every success in your endeavors. Teaching is a most extraordinary and fulfilling profession. We continue to be awed by how it has enriched our own lives and given us the gift of possibly enriching the lives of others. If you come to it prepared, and willing to remain a learner as well as a teacher, we are sure it will do the same for you.

To the Instructor

Instructors using previous editions of this book will find that the text has been extensively revised. However, the three approaches and the core notions that constitute them are very much as they were developed in the previous three editions. The main differences in this edition are as follows: (1) the formula *TØSxy* and the Educated Person (EP) card have been eliminated in favor of the MAKER framework; (2) the therapist (first and second editions) or fostering (third edition) approach has been renamed the *facilitator* approach; (3) care pedagogy is treated as a variation on the facilitator approach and emancipationist teaching is treated as a variation on the liberationist approach; (4) objections to the different approaches are now treated together in chapter 5; and (5) readers are encouraged to gain an understanding of and experience with all three approaches rather than to choose a single approach.

APPROACHES
to TEACHING

Chapter 1

Approaches to Teaching

This is a book about different approaches to teaching. Its purpose is to stimulate you to think about some basic ways to conceive of the role of the teacher. We believe that the approach you take to your teaching has a great effect on what you do as a teacher. To help you see what we mean, we begin with a sketch of the way three very different, yet quite effective, teachers teach. You may have had teachers like these yourself. Their ways of approaching teaching can be found in practice in any subject and on any grade level, even though here we have located them across a spectrum of subjects and grades. As you read about them, ask yourself: What makes them different? What is the main goal of their teaching? Do you find one teacher's approach more appealing than the others? Is one a better fit with your own intuitions about good teaching?

Three Teachers

Jim Barnes has taught a number of different lower grades in the Bryant Elementary School over the past twelve years. The children like him. He is always firm and in command, but also kind and gentle. Jim believes that his contribution to the education of these youngsters is to give them both a set of basic skills that will be useful to them all their lives and a knowledge of specific subject matter that will allow them to successfully progress through their schooling and eventually become productively engaged in a democratic society.

He has experimented with a lot of different curriculum materials, but the ones he likes best and finds to be most effective share a number of common characteristics. They are highly organized and systematic, so the children can follow them easily. Because of the materials' logical sequencing, the children are able to quickly develop useful patterns and strategies for dealing with them. The materials are progressive; that is, the children need what they learn today to be able to do the work tomorrow. Each new learning builds on the last and leads to the next. Jim also relies on numerous nonthreatening evaluations so he can know exactly how each child is doing, what each needs help with, and when each is ready to move on. He prides himself on being a very efficient and effective teacher.

Most important, the children have a sense of accomplishment. They pride themselves on their achievements, and more than a few have stretched their parents' patience by insisting on reciting the whole of the multiplication tables or the Gettysburg Address, showing how they can solve ten difficult math problems, or classifying all living creatures in appropriate zoological categories. There is a spirit of "can-do" in Jim's classes. He leads and directs enthusiastically; he manages and executes skillfully; he judges and evaluates fairly. The materials make sense, and the work is doable. Jim is a successful teacher.

Nancy Kwong is also successful at what she does. She teaches English to middle school adolescents who are just beginning to discover who they are as persons. Nancy believes that the most important thing an education can give to youngsters is some perspective on themselves, on who and what they are, on who and what they might become. She teaches as if each word of literature they read was written for them and was connected to their own life experiences. She finds that journal writing provides a real outlet for feelings and personal perspectives, helping them to grow and develop, as well as a vehicle for encouraging a student's ability to communicate and write effectively.

Books are chosen by her students because they are about something *they* want to read about. There is no set curriculum. Any of the books in the school library are fair game. Class discussions are genuine dialogues, the sharing of reading experiences by equals. Nancy does not run the class as much as she runs with it. She shares her own perspectives and values with her students; they see her as a sympathetic, understanding, encouraging adult, unlike most of the other adults in their lives. They also see her as a teacher who cares about them as well as about the subject matter. There is no doubt about her love for literature and poetry. It shines in her eyes. There is no doubt in their minds either that she respects each one of them equally. It shows in her genuine interactions with each student. Nancy feels good about her nurturing relationship with young learners.

Roberto Umbras teaches history and social studies in an urban high school that is beset by the many problems of the inner city. For many, however, his classes are an island of calm in a sea of trouble. Racial and ethnic tension abound in his school. Roberto understands and respects cultural differences and tries to help his students do the same. He is, however, primarily a historian. His love for history began at an early age, and as he progressed through his studies, he came to the realization that the best way to learn history is to learn to be a historian. So that is how he approaches all his classes. Roberto believes that education should be an initiation into the many ways human beings have developed to make sense of their world. History and math, science and literature, music and art, all of the subjects are ways of knowing. The theories and methods of the social sciences, for example, are ways we have developed to understand the social world, and the skills and techniques of the historian help us unravel and make sense of our collective past.

His students quickly sense the difference in Roberto's classes. He treats them as people who can think, who can have valid opinions and ideas. They quickly learn, however, that ideas and opinions need to be backed up by facts. Historians cannot just tell interesting stories; they have to provide evidence for their claims and interpretations. Perhaps the most exciting thing they learn is that there is not just one true history. There are histories written from different national, cultural, and ethnic perspectives. There are different interpretations of the same historical event. History is written by human beings trying to make sense of the past, and no one is completely free of bias of some sort.

Roberto models the historian at work in many of his classes and asks his students to do the same. They collect primary materials and secondary sources dealing with an event or period of time. Conjectures and hypotheses are generated, and the materials are mined to see if sufficient data can be found to support the students' fledgling interpretations. Students really appreciate reading diaries and letters, other firsthand accounts, and official reports. It makes history come alive for many for the first time. While few if any of them will ever become historians, they have, Roberto feels, an appreciation of the past, of differences in interpretation and cultural perspectives, and of a way to think and support claims made about human events. His students feel enabled.

How would you characterize the approaches of each of these teachers? Jim is trying to convey basic subject matter and skills as efficiently as possible. Nancy is trying to nurture the personhood of her students by engaging them in meaningful experiences that connect with their lives. Roberto is trying to get his students to think as historians do and to understand the way we try to make sense of the past. We could have exchanged these approaches across grade levels and subjects. For example, Jim's approach could be used in high school history. Nancy's approach could be used in Jim's elementary classes. And Roberto's approach could be used in middle school literature classes.

The important thing to realize here is that how teachers view their role and goals as teachers has a considerable impact on how they structure their teaching. In this book, we will help you explore and think about three very basic approaches to teaching. For convenience, we have named them the *executive*, the *facilitator*, and the *liberationist* approaches, although they go by many names. Each has its historical roots as well as its contemporary research and scholarly support structure. But most important, each offers you a way to probe into your own intuitions about what you as a teacher should do.

The Amazing Glasses

It is important to remember, however, that these approaches are *conceptions* of teaching. They are ideas about what teaching is and should be. As such, they are also open to appraisal and criticism, adoption, rejection, or modification. They are three different perspectives that contemporary educators have used to conceive of the activity of teaching in ways that they think will help us do it better. Indeed, in this sense, they are more like lenses through which to explore and understand the various activities of teaching than they are hard-and-fast categories for how to teach. This lens analogy is so helpful in thinking about the approaches to teaching that we want to expand on it with a fanciful story.

Imagine sitting on the porch of a farmhouse with a panoramic view of the farmland in front of you. On a table beside your chair are three pairs of glasses. Curious, you try on a pair. Amazingly, you see the work being done by all the farm implements, from the hand tools to the heavy machinery. You watch in great fascination, having long wondered what the different pieces of equipment do and how things all work together to get from seed to harvested crop. After gazing in awe for some time, you remember that there are two other pairs of glasses on the table. You put on the second pair. Before you now are all the creatures in the fields, from the tiny aphid to the garter snakes and rabbits. Again you are amazed to see more than wildlife here; you see how the food chain works, both in terms of how these creatures are interdependent with the crops that form their habitat as well as the predator-prey relationships that define the terms of their existence. You want to keep these glasses on, yet the wonder of what the third pair might reveal beckons you to switch.

Reluctantly, you take off the second pair and don the third. Arrayed before you is the human side of the farm: the executives of the corporation that owns it, the members of the family that manages it, the permanent workers who labor here throughout the year, and the migrant workers who come when the crops are ready to harvest. You see more than the people, however; you see the connections that define their working relationships, as well as how good and bad management practices affect the quality of work performed and the overall productivity of the farm. You watch for a while, then take off the third pair of glasses and switch back to the second, then to the first, and later back to the third. You are filled with fascination. What a way to learn about farming, to come to grasp its mechanical, biological, and social dimensions in all their complexities—yet with the relative ease of looking through three pairs of glasses and noting with care what you see.

Some weeks later, you find yourself in the back of a classroom, observing a teacher and her students. You think you have a rough sense of what is going on, but you're just not sure. Would it not be helpful if there were three pairs of glasses on the desk next to you and you could just put them on to see clearly and deeply into all that is taking place here? That is just what we propose to offer you: a metaphorical three pairs of glasses through which to view and understand different approaches to teaching. Of course, we also hope to be offering you a way to enrich your own conception of the role, purposes, and persona you want to be yours as a teacher.

Three Approaches to Teaching

The first approach, the teacher as executive, views the teacher as a manager of complex classroom processes, a person charged with bringing about certain outcomes with students through using the best skills and techniques available. Carefully developed curriculum materials and methods of teaching backed by research are very important to this approach. They provide the teacher with techniques and understandings to use in the management of the classroom and the production of learning. Jim Barnes probably was using this approach.

The facilitator approach is the second of the three approaches. It places a high value on what students bring to the classroom setting. It places considerable emphasis on making use of students' prior experience. The facilitative teacher is typically an empathetic person who believes in helping individuals grow personally and reach a high level of self-actualization and self-understanding. Humanistic psychology, learning theory, and existential philosophy are some of the fields of scholarship that underwrite this view.[1] Nancy Kwong exemplifies this approach.

The liberationist approach, the third and final approach, views the teacher as one who frees and opens the mind of the learner, initiating him or her into human ways of knowing and assisting the learner in becoming a well-rounded, knowledgeable, and moral human being. The classical idea of a liberal education underwrites the mainstream version of this approach.[2] Roberto Umbras appears to be engaged in this approach.

Although there is much to learn about these different approaches to teaching, it is, of course, possible to teach without thinking about one's approach. Just as one can be a lover or a parent without giving much thought to the meaning of love or the responsibilities of parenting, one can teach without engaging in deep reflection on the nature and purpose of the activity. But we believe that teachers become professionals only when they reflect on and choose a stance toward their calling that guides and sustains them in the important work of educating persons. We also believe that, in this instance, knowledge is power. Possessing an understanding of different approaches to teaching provides you with a basis for reflection on and appraisal of your work. Even more rewarding, it gives you the power to choose ways to teach that will help you achieve one of the noblest goals to which human beings can aspire: assisting the young in becoming thoughtful, competent, and caring adults.

The amazing-glasses metaphor captures well the use of the three approaches as ways to study and reflect on teaching. However, to bring the three approaches closer to home, we also treat them as if they were styles of teaching for you to try on. Our purpose here is twofold. First, to provide you with a means with which to analyze and reflect upon the teachers you observe, and second, to provide you with an opportunity to ponder a style of teaching that seems right for you. This dual use means that you will sometimes find us using the three approaches as devices for analyzing the activities of teaching and other times treating the approaches as teaching styles that you might adopt as your own.

Even though the three approaches are not, in each and every respect, completely separable from one another, we present them in ways designed to highlight the differences between them. As will become evident, the three approaches share quite a few features, despite their differences. In the following three chapters we will present the approaches by highlighting the maximum contrast between them. Then, in chapter 5, we will reconsider these contrasting properties.

The book concludes with a chapter devoted entirely to cases and disputes. As you complete your reading of each chapter, we urge you to make extensive use of these cases and disputes to stimulate and focus your thinking about important issues and applications of the three approaches. For example, the case "Go Fly a Kite" at the end of chapter 7 provides an opportunity to see how three teachers at the same grade level approach the same class project quite differently. Will you please turn to it now, so that you have an idea of what we are talking about?

As you will see from your reading of the "Go Fly a Kite" case, the cases are a very important means for you to dig more deeply into the ideas behind each of the three approaches as well as to discover where you stand relative to the different approaches. Thinking them through before discussing them with fellow students will assist you in sorting through your own points of view; subsequently, discussing them with fellow students will enlarge both your understanding and your perspective. If past experience with these cases is any guide, you will be amazed at the great range of differences between your classmates.

The Common Framework: MAKER

Before we turn to examining each of the three approaches in depth, it will prove helpful to have a means to compare and contrast the different approaches. What we are calling the MAKER framework serves this purpose. This framework consists of the five core elements of teaching. They are *Method*, *Awareness* of students, *Knowledge* of the content, *Ends* that describe the purposes and ideals for teaching, and the *Relationship* that exists between the teacher and students.

These five elements are common to all teaching. No matter what level you teach, or where and how you do so, your work can be described using these five elements. As a guide to memory, we have arranged the first letter of these elements to form the acronym MAKER (always in uppercase letters in this book).

Each of the three approaches to teaching—executive, facilitator, liberationist—has its own MAKER profile. That is, each approach has its own variation on two or more of the five elements. It is worth our while to spend a few moments exploring each of the five elements.

The first element, Method (*M*), pertains to the skills and techniques teachers use to assist students in gaining the knowledge, understanding, and skill that teachers intend their students to achieve. Included within this dimension are such things as how lessons are planned, how the classroom is organized, how tasks and duties are devised and assigned to various students, how new material is structured and conveyed and old material refreshed, how student work is judged, and how these judgments are communicated to students and to their parents. You may have noticed that the dominant word in this list of examples is *how*. For the most part, Method pertains to how you teach (the fourth element, Ends, pertains to *why* you teach as you do, but more on that in a moment).

Awareness (*A*) is the second in the framework of common elements. It is quite straightforward, for it refers to what the teacher knows about his or her students, including such things as their interests, talents, and concerns; their personal histories and family backgrounds; and their performance in previous years of schooling. Awareness, in this context, is not about "real time" awareness, such as when a teacher becomes aware that a student is about to do something he or she should not do. Awareness as we use it here refers to what and how much the teacher knows about the students.

The third element, Knowledge (*K*), covers what a teacher knows about the subject matter she is teaching. If she is a teacher of science, for instance, how well does she know science? How firm is her grasp of the important concepts, theories, and facts? Is she comfortable with the methods of in-quiry that are common to the various disciplines within the sciences? Is her understanding of the subject matter sufficiently deep that she can explain it using metaphors and analogies that make the content more accessible to students without distorting its integrity and validity?

Ends (*E*), the fourth element, are the purposes a teacher has for his teaching and for his students. Ends are revealed in the answers to such questions as the following: What do you want your students to know and be able to do? What are you trying to accomplish as a teacher? What are your ideal educational aims? Although all five of the MAKER elements can be slippery to interpret, Ends is perhaps the trickiest. That is because we often draw a distinction between the ends of education and the ends of schooling. Did that last sentence cause you to pause, wondering what we could possibly mean by distinguishing schooling from education? The dif-ference between the two becomes increasingly important as we move from executive to facilitator to liberationist.

In this book, when we write of the ends of education, we refer to the grand and noble ideals that we seek for the children and youth who attend the nation's schools. These ends should be distinguished from two other phenomena with which they are often confused. The first of these are the goals of schooling, which are the specific outcomes we hope schooling will accomplish. The second are the actual consequences of schooling, which may or may not be congruent with either the goals or the ends.

This three-way distinction may seem a bit confusing at first, but it is well worth your while to master it. Ends are the high ideals we hold for the education of the young; goals are the specific outcomes we hope the young will attain as a result of their schooling; consequences are the actual results obtained from the experience of schooling. As an example, a community might hold ends that include the cultivation of critical thinking, moral rec-titude, and exemplary citizenship. It may set as the goals of schooling learning to read, write, problem solve, and master bodies of knowledge from different subject areas. The consequences of schooling—what children actually take away from the experience—may be considerably different from either the ends or the goals.

The importance of the distinction between ends, goals, and conse-quences is that they can nestle harmoniously with one another or they can be in opposition to one another. The desired state of affairs, of course, is to have all three aligned with one another, such that they are mutually rein-forcing. Such a state of affairs is far from easy to obtain, as our exploration of the various approaches to teaching will make clear. Unfortunately, it seems that it is more often the case that the ends, goals, and consequences work against one another. As we examine the various approaches, we will illustrate how this tension arises and what would be required to resolve it.

The fifth and last element, Relationships (*R*), covers the kind of connection that teachers forge with their students. Do you, for example, believe that student mastery of subject matter is the paramount consideration and that this mastery is best obtained by your remaining somewhat aloof from students' personal interests and concerns? Perhaps, by contrast, you believe that you cannot be the teacher you want to be without becoming a friend and caring guide to your students. From yet another perspective, you might have the sense that to succeed with your students, you will need to "get inside their heads" to see how they think and respond, so that you can better assist them to become powerful critical thinkers and moral deliberators. Each of these represents a different way to develop relationships with your students, ways that you will find featured in the different approaches to teaching.

Using MAKER with the Approaches

As each approach is presented, you will see that some elements are prominent features of one approach while other elements are less so. The elements are like dominant and recessive genes: Some are dominant in one approach to teaching but recessive in another approach. If you happen to play bridge, you can think of the elements as suits in the deck, with some being trump in one approach but not in another. For example, *M* and *K* are dominant in the executive approach, while *A* and *R* are dominant in the facilitator approach. It is our hope that this way of comparing the approaches will deepen your understanding of them.

One last thought before we turn to the executive approach: Another value of the MAKER framework is that all the elements are under your control. For example, you make the decision of how thorough your understanding of Method will be; you also decide on the various skills and techniques you will employ in the classroom. You have the option to decide how Aware you will become of the life experiences and character of your students and how this understanding will affect your teaching. You have control over how thoroughly prepared you will be in the subjects you teach, and how you will represent your Knowledge to your students. You have considerable freedom to adopt Ends for your teaching, and to pursue them in your classroom. Finally, the kind of Relationship you have with your students and how this Relationship complements or detracts from your efforts is very much up to you.

Think of MAKER not only as a framework for comparing and contrasting approaches to teaching, but also as domains of expertise, such that the more knowledgeable and proficient you become in any domain, the better teacher you are likely to be. The three approaches to teaching presented here offer different perspectives on what elements or domains are crucially important to good teaching and on why it is important for you to master these elements.

Before going on to the following chapter, you should look at the pertinent cases in chapter 7, particularly "Grading Policies" and "School and Approach Mismatch." Doing so will give you a chance to examine your own predispositions toward the different approaches as well as help you see how a teacher's approach to teaching might conflict with school policy and cause problems. We hope you will also get the sense that doing serious thinking about the different approaches is not just an academic exercise; it is crucial to helping you become the kind of teacher we are sure you want to be.

Chapter 2

The Executive Approach

Classrooms are complex places. Often twenty-five to thirty-five children are contained in a confined space, along with a teacher and perhaps an aide. There is a great deal going on. The children are there because they are required to be there, and the teacher is trying to engage the students in the study of whatever content is prescribed. The complexity of classrooms, when joined with the demand that certain things take place there, means that they must in some way be managed.

Managing Your Classroom

How do you manage a classroom? Think about it. Your task is to engage the students in academic work of some sort. To do that, you have to determine what they are to be taught (curriculum guides might help here). Then you must figure out whether the students in your classroom are able (ready) to learn what is prescribed for them. After you have diagnosed the students to determine their readiness for the material you want to present, you may find that they are not quite up to it. You may have to revise the material, adapting it to make it more accessible to them. Once you have the material ready, you have to figure out how to get it across. What motivational devices might be used to interest the students and keep them engaged? What classroom structure best contributes to successful learning—small groups, large groups, whole-class instruction, or independent learning?

And this is only the *planning* stage. After you figure out what is to be done, then you must do it. No matter how well you plan, events will occur that cause you to veer from your plan. In the course of teaching, you are constantly making decisions about the students, the material, and the overall success or failure of your efforts. You probably will revise your plan many times while on your feet teaching the lesson.

Then after you teach it, you may follow up with an evaluation, only to find that a mere six out of twenty-eight students understood more than half of what you taught. Now you have to reteach the unit, but you are stymied about how to reconstruct it so that most of the students will understand it. Extensive reflection is called for here, on both what has already happened and what should happen next.

All this complexity requires careful planning, action carried out on the basis of the plan (with many revisions en route), then follow-up evaluation, revised plans, and another instructional effort. These are the kinds of things that executives do. They manage people and resources through planning, action, assessment, and reaction on the basis of experience and evidence. Executives make decisions about what people will do, when they will do it, how long it is likely to take, what standard of performance will be attained, and what happens if these standards are not met.

Until recently, very little thought was given to the teacher as an executive. On the contrary, teachers were thought simply to be experts in the subjects they taught, while students were willing participants in the teaching of these subjects. The task of teaching seemed fairly straightforward: Just get the youngsters together, gain their attention, present a well-constructed lesson, and you could go home knowing that you did a day's work well. This view prevailed for a good part of the nineteenth and twentieth centuries. Then, beginning in the 1970s, researchers began careful and extensive studies of actual classroom settings. They found them far more complex than the folk wisdom of the time had led most people to believe. And they found teachers engaged in more complex and sophisticated endeavors than they had traditionally been given credit for.

As our understanding of the complexity of the classroom situation emerged from research on teaching,[1] it became clear that teachers were more than subject-matter experts with interesting gimmicks for getting that subject matter across to their students. What the researchers found were teachers who managed classroom aides, dealt with concerned parents, responded to school administrators who sometimes intervened in classrooms in unhelpful ways, coped with textbooks and supplementary materials that were often inappropriate for the students they served, and spent great amounts of time complying with policy mandates from local, state, and federal regulations—all this, plus teaching content to students in their classes.

Managing Time in the Classroom

Not surprisingly, researchers were impressed that teachers faced all these tasks and pressures and handled them with varying degrees of success. Some researchers (particularly David Berliner[2]) found the metaphor of the executive to be an accurate and helpful one to use in understanding the work of a teacher. However, it was not simply the pressure and complexity of the classroom that made the executive metaphor appealing. Something else emerged from the early studies of teachers. It seemed that effective teaching might be analyzed into a discrete set of generic, or common, skills. That is, regardless of the grade level, the nature of the students, the subject matter, or the culture of the school, certain instructional practices seemed to be regularly associated with gains in student achievement, while other instructional practices appeared unrelated to student mastery of content. Discrete executive skills for teaching could be identified.

For example, the practice of engaging in friendly chit-chat with the class—discussing ball games, the national news, or the gossip around school—is *not* a practice associated with gains in student learning. Indeed, the avoidance of academic work in classrooms has been the subject of several fascinating studies, wherein researchers have noted that teachers and students forge "treaties" or "bargains" to sidestep rigorous academic work in favor of relaxed and pleasant relationships in the classroom.[3] Although the concept of student-teacher treaties was not developed when the studies on instructional time began, the absence of academic work was evident enough to alert Berliner and other researchers to the importance of the time variable in student learning.[4] They rediscovered a very simple idea: By and large, students learn what they study, and how much they learn is in large measure determined by how much time they are engaged in that study.

Not surprising, is it? What is surprising is the way teachers dealt with time. Consider a distinction that comes from one of the most well known instructional time studies, the Beginning Teacher Evaluation Study (BTES).[5] BTES researchers distinguished between *allocated* time and *engaged* time. Allocated time is how much time a teacher or school sets aside for the study of some subject. Engaged time is the time a given student actually works at the subject. What the researchers found is that elementary schools and teachers varied widely in allocated time for the different subjects. Some teachers would, for example, allocate forty-five minutes a day to math, while others would allocate thirty minutes; some would allocate thirty-five minutes to science, others would hardly touch science study; some teachers always devoted forty to fifty minutes a day to social studies, while others would allocate zero to fifteen minutes to it some days and sixty to ninety minutes on other days.

Clearly, the amount of time allocated to a subject makes a tremendous difference in students' opportunity to learn it. If the teacher does not spend much time with math, then it is not surprising that his or her students fare poorly on math exams. However, this variation in allocated time was not the big surprise in the research on instructional time. The big surprise was in engaged time. By focusing on selected students in a classroom, the researchers clocked the amount of time in which these target students were engaged in the assigned activity, or "on-task." What they found was that even though a teacher might allocate fifty minutes to math, a student might be on-task only seven or eight of those fifty minutes! The engaged time for a given student might be less than 20 percent of the allocated time.

Consider the impact of this finding. If, in general, students learn subject content only if they study it, and the amount of that learning is directly related to the amount of time spent studying (the more you study the more you learn, generally speaking), then in order to learn something well, it is necessary to spend a fair amount of time with it. However, by looking at selected students, it was found that some students spent as few as seven out of fifty minutes actually engaged in the academic tasks assigned by the teacher. How could this happen? It is far easier to slip up than you might think. Consider this example.

You set aside fifty minutes for the math unit. It begins right after recess, which ends at 10:35 A.M. The students do not get back at the same time, so you wait until they are all in their seats. Time: 10:39. There are some announcements and a few things you want them to know about activities taking place this afternoon and later in the week. Time: 10:41. There is an outburst in the back of the room. You settle that. Time: 10:42. You start the math lesson with some directions about a task you want everybody to do in his or her workbook, saying that they should take ten minutes for this assignment and then the whole class will discuss it. You spend some time explaining how you want students to do the task. These instructions are not teaching them anything about math, only about how to complete the workbook pages. Time: 10:46. Eleven minutes gone and no math activity has occurred yet.

At last the students are working in the books. It so happens that Harry, however, did not really understand your instructions. Because he is rather shy, he does not raise his hand for help. It is 10:49 before you notice him doodling in the margin of the book. You walk back to his desk and clear up the confusion; he begins to work fifteen minutes after the scheduled beginning of the math period. Within two minutes, he is confused. He puzzles over the difficulty for a while, then stops working. It is 10:53 and Harry is off-task again. You are busy with the other students, so do not notice his problem. He is too embarrassed to ask for help, especially since he thought you were a bit impatient with him the time before. He waits until you start class discussion to learn the solution to the problem that threw him off. You are a little late getting the group started in discussion. It is 10:58 before the discussion begins.

Harry goes back on-task at the beginning of the discussion and stays with you for the duration of the discussion, which concludes at 11:11. Thus he was on-task for thirteen minutes of the discussion plus two minutes during the workbook exercise. Thirty-six minutes of allocated time have elapsed, and Harry has accumulated fifteen minutes of engaged time. You have a chance to increase the percentage of Harry's engaged time by managing the remaining fourteen minutes of allocated time so that Harry can be actively involved in the content of the lesson. But that does not happen, because you look at the clock and note that it is 11:11 and that the period is scheduled to end at 11:25. You conclude that it is not worthwhile for you to begin another unit with so little time remaining, so you assign the students to their workbooks in order to fill the remaining time.

Harry works productively for three more minutes, then becomes stumped again. You are not monitoring student seatwork, however, as you are busy completing the attendance report, which is due in the school office in five minutes. Hence you overlook the fact that Harry has been gazing out the window for some time. At 11:25 you call the math period to a halt. Harry has been on-task in the study of math for only eighteen of the fifty minutes, just about 35 percent of the available time. Not good, but how much engaged time do you think the other students in your class had? It is quite possible that some of your students had even less engaged time than Harry, while others had more.

Features of This Approach

Researchers have found that there are many ways for teachers to increase the time in which students are engaged. These skills for managing learning time are considered generic teaching skills, because they appear to be unrelated to student background characteristics such as race or home environment, to the subject matter taught, or to the nature of the school setting. These time-management skills are intended to increase the percentage of engaged time relative to allocated time, and include such techniques as monitoring seatwork, reducing idle chatter, maintaining a down-to-business atmosphere, and providing students with an easy, comfortable means to signal their confusion with material under consideration.

Time engaged in academic work is not, however, the only aspect of the executive approach to teaching. Among the many other methods or techniques are three that appear to have a major impact on the effectiveness of a teacher's efforts.[6] They are cues, corrective feedback, and reinforcement. Cues are like maps and signposts; the teacher employs them to alert students to what is to be learned and how to go about learning it. Teachers who make extensive use of cues, particularly in the early segments of an instructional sequence, often have a stronger impact on learning than those who do not use cues. The same can be said for corrective feedback, wherein teachers quickly remedy errors in written and oral work. Reinforcement, ranging from a fleeting smile through comments on homework assignments all the way to such tangible rewards as food, toys, or money, is also quite powerful as an instructional technique, although it requires experience and insight into the learner for it to be employed well.

Another aspect of the executive approach is known as *opportunity to learn*—giving students the chance to learn what is being taught. Sometimes teachers embark on complex topics or ideas but allow too little opportunity for students to become involved in these topics to the extent that the topics demand. The material is covered too quickly, without adequate background preparation, or is misrepresented in order to cover it in the short time allowed. Any of these factors denies the student adequate opportunity to learn the material.

One of the generic skills frequently associated with opportunity to learn is known as "wait time." It is generally understood as the time that elapses between a teacher's question and a student's response to that question. All too often, teachers fail to allow sufficient wait time, especially with questions that call for a good deal of critical thought. One of our favorite examples is the teacher who asks, "How might the history of the United States be different if its colonization had occurred from west to east rather than east to west?" The wait time for such a powerful question might reasonably be several minutes, as students ponder all the variables and permutations at work in this inquiry. Unfortunately, many teachers become impatient if no one responds within a few seconds, and they proceed to answer the question for the students.

Wait time provides a good example of some of the tensions that arise in the executive approach to teaching. As we have seen, managing time to optimize engagement is vital to the executive approach. At the same time, one of the generic skills vital to this approach, wait time, calls for allowing long pauses so that students have ample opportunity to think through complex issues or problems. The tension might be resolved by allowing the necessary wait time, but in a way that ensures that as many students as possible are engaged in mulling over the problem as thoroughly as possible. Although it may sound easy enough to do, it requires considerable skill. This is another way of indicating that teaching seems to call for the skills of an executive in order for it to be done well.

There is an interesting facet to all these features of the executive approach to teaching. They all place a high premium on student learning. What is so strange about that? Is not student learning what schools and teachers are all about? Well, yes . . . but should everything a teacher does be determined by what advances student learning of selected subject matter? What about nurturing a strong bond between teacher and student? What about helping the student to develop his or her own strengths and interests? What about fostering the moral capacities of the student? The best way to come to grips with these questions is to use the MAKER framework to analyze the executive approach.

The MAKER Framework

You will recall from the previous chapter that MAKER is our acronym for the five core elements of any teaching endeavor: Methods of teaching,

Awareness of students, Knowledge of the subject matter, Ends that guide teaching and learning, and Relationships between teacher and students. Each of the three major approaches to teaching described in this book emphasizes some of the five elements while giving less attention to others. Hence the MAKER framework is not only a useful device for explaining each of the approaches; it is a valuable means for distinguishing between the three approaches. To begin to see how this works, let's look carefully at the executive approach.

In capsule summary, the executive stresses M and K (Methods of teaching and Knowledge of subject matter) and places comparatively less emphasis on A (Awareness of one's students), E (Ends that guide the activities of teaching and learning), and R (Relationships between teacher and students). That said, we pause here to make an important point: All three approaches described in this book attend in some way to all five elements. But they do so differently, often by shifting the degree of emphasis or assigning a different meaning to one or more of the elements. Take Knowledge, for example. It is one of the most diversely interpreted elements across the three approaches.

Knowledge of subject matter is an element that applies to both teacher and student. That is, it refers to how knowledgeable the teacher is with respect to the subject matter being taught as well as to what the student knows about the subject, following instruction. Behind both of these lie theories about what counts as knowledge, how we come to acquire it, and what it means to be mistaken or deceived about what we think we know. You might, at first blush, wonder how relevant such theories could be to teaching, but the applications are immense. In the executive approach, for instance, knowledge (K) is typically treated as something "out there," external to the teacher and the learner, with the teacher serving as a conveyor of that knowledge to the student. For the executive, the student arrives in the classroom relatively or completely uninformed—without K—and the teacher manages complex instructional processes that enable the student to acquire K (from such sources as texts, films, the Internet, workbooks, teacher presentations, discussions, and so forth).

As we shall see in the following two chapters, the K element functions differently in the facilitator and liberationist approaches. Briefly stated, and as is explained in more detail in the coming chapters, the facilitative teacher views the student as coming to the classroom already in possession of a good deal of K, with the task of the teacher to assist the student to both become aware of this K and link it to new K that is being acquired in the setting of the school. The liberationist teacher has a view of K that is related to that of the executive, but holds a quite different view not only of how to acquire it, but also of what ends (E) are served by possessing K. For the liberationist, K is not an end itself, but a means of initiating the student into the accumulated wisdom and understanding of the human race for the purpose of advancing the species.

Did you notice how *E* (Ends) slipped into these descriptions? That's because the *E* element is emphasized by the facilitator and the liberationist (but in quite different ways), while it is assumed by the executive to be simply the acquisition of *K*. In other words, acquiring *K* is the primary end of the executive approach, while the facilitator and liberationist approaches stipulate ends that go well beyond the acquisition of subject-matter knowledge. But enough of these comparisons; we'll do more of that in chapter 5. Let's finish the analysis of the executive.

Given the executive's emphasis on the efficient and effective management of classroom processes, it comes as no surprise that the Methods element (*M*) is central to this approach. The core concern for the executive is to use *M* to get *K* across to the students. Among these methods are those generic skills previously discussed, including time management, cues, corrective feedback, reinforcement, and wait time. Other means often employed by the executive are a highly structured curriculum, elaborately scripted lesson plans, and rigorous testing.

While the executive attends with considerable care to the study and improvement of methods, knowledge (*K*) is often treated as a given. It is what is set forth in the adopted curriculum, and what appears in textbooks, workbooks, and other learning aids. Its form and composition are frequently determined by state-mandated curriculum guides (check the websites of almost any state department of education to see what these look like) and by the tests that students must pass to advance from grade to grade or to graduate. Thus while *K* is central to the executive approach, it is not studied and developed in the way *M* is.

Although not ignored in the executive approach, *A*, *E*, and *R* are given little attention in their own right. Rather, they are studied as instrumental elements, that is, as elements whose value rests on what they might contribute to the student's learning of *K*. As such, one does not hear a great deal of discussion within the executive approach about coming to know one's students well (*A*), or about the forging of strong and powerful bonds between teacher and students (*R*). With regard to *E*, it has already been pointed out that the executive merges *E* with *K* by asserting that the proper end of education is for the student to acquire *K*.

A strength of the executive approach is that it provides a very clear, straightforward means to move some specified knowledge from a source (for example, a book, teacher, or computer) to the mind of the learner. Indeed, if followed with care, the executive approach increases the probability that more of the students will learn more of the content than would otherwise be the case. As one prominent researcher put it, "Teacher effectiveness refers to the ability of a classroom teacher to produce higher than predicted gains on standardized achievement tests."[7] Why is it important that *K* be moved from source to student as efficiently and effectively as possible? Just a bit of recent history answers this question and throws a great deal of light on the executive approach to teaching.

Before turning to this history, we would like to stress that such historical background is important to you, as a teacher, because having an historical sense of why things are the way they are in schools is one of your best aids for understanding what's happening now and how you might work to improve it.

Historical Roots

The notion that an effective teacher is one who produces powerful gains in student achievement (as measured by standardized tests) is an idea barely past the age of majority. Its beginnings can be traced back to the stimulus-response-reward psychology of Edward L. Thorndike in the early twentieth century. Thorndike's ideas were later revised and extended by the famous behavioral psychologist B. F. Skinner, whose work was to have a powerful impact on educational practice. In 1954, in a paper suggestively titled "The Science of Learning and the Art of Teaching," Skinner contended that "the whole process of becoming competent in any field must be divided into a very large number of very small steps, and reinforcement must be contingent upon the accomplishment of each step."[8] Ten years later, he stated the point even more boldly: "The application of operant conditioning to education is simple and direct. Teaching is the arrangement of contingencies of reinforcement under which students learn."[9] In simple terms, teachers could bring about the learning they sought from students by knowing precisely when and how to reward students for behaviors that increasingly approximated the goals set for them.

Skinner's contentions about teaching and learning set the stage for two things. First, they encouraged many educators to strip away much of the mystique about teaching as an ineffable human activity. Second, they led educational researchers to draw a tighter loop around the interaction between teacher and learner. The notion of teaching as stimulus, or cause, and learning as response, or effect, enabled researchers to focus exclusively on these two behaviors without becoming sidetracked by the family backgrounds of students, students' life histories, or the particular subject matter to be learned. Skinner's work had a powerful effect on the conceptions that many of us have about teaching and learning and about how the former affects the latter.

These conceptions might have had far less influence on the actual practice of education, were it not for some events taking place in the political and economic sectors of our society at the time. Following the *Brown v.*

Board of Education decision in 1954, the federal government made ever-increasing commitments to schooling as an instrument for the eradication of social inequalities. These commitments reached a very high intensity in the mid-1960s with President Lyndon B. Johnson's Great Society programs, such as Head Start, Follow Through, and Parent-Child Centers. As more and more dollars were channeled into education, policy makers became increasingly curious about how the money was being spent and whether it was actually helping the students to whom it was targeted.

As part of the Civil Rights Act of 1964, Congress mandated a study of equal educational opportunity among various racial and ethnic groups. This study was directed by James Coleman and is most frequently referred to as the Coleman Report.[10] Its purpose was to examine the relationship between various factors and educational achievement. Using a massive sample of 600,000 students, 60,000 teachers, and 4,000 schools, Coleman found that the amount of money spent on schools did not seem to make much difference in the achievement of those who attended them. He found that different racial groups attended different schools, that the physical differences between these schools were not all that great, that such differences in facilities and professional personnel that he could find did not make much difference in what students accomplished, and that White students often learned far more in their schools than students belonging to other racial and ethnic groups learned in theirs.

The preceding sentence says a great deal and warrants a second reading. According to Coleman, equality of educational achievement was not obtained by making educational facilities equal. It is, rather, the background of the students (particularly parents' income and educational levels) that affects educational attainment in the setting of the school. Coleman's data indicated that student peers had a far stronger influence on educational attainment (or lack of it) than did the quality of the school's physical facilities, the richness of its curriculum, or the preparation of its teachers. These findings were devastating for educators, who thought that they and their schools had a dramatic impact on student learning.

To understand exactly what is going on here, we have to look at the notion of variance in student achievement. We know, for example, that in 1964 Blacks and Whites, as groups, varied dramatically in what they learned in school. Once this fact is acknowledged, then the question becomes, What accounts for this large variation in student achievement? Coleman argued that family background and peer influence accounted for most of the variance and that schools and teachers had little effect on the variance. That was the conclusion that bothered educators, cast doubt on Great Society programs, and led those who controlled educational dollars to look harder at how they were being spent.

Teaching for Student Achievement

After the initial shock of the Coleman Report, researchers began to find flaws in it. The first questions raised were about the statistical procedures used to analyze the data; then the design of the study was disputed; and, inevitably, the validity of the conclusions became suspect. New research programs were begun, programs that were particularly directed at finding out whether Coleman was correct. This research was shaped in large part by the behaviorists' cause-and-effect conception of teaching and learning. Researchers viewed teaching as a discrete set of behaviors and tried to discover whether different sets of behaviors were related to different learning gains by students. These researchers assumed a tight connection between teaching as a cause and learning as an effect that follows from teaching. The researchers were not burdened with fancy ideas about the nobility of teaching, nor did they pay much attention to the so-called inputs of education (such as the size of the school library, per-pupil expenditure, or the number of college recruiters who visited the school in a year). On the contrary, they went straight for the jugular. They had one burning question: Do the instructional behaviors of some teachers lead to systematic gains in student achievement, while different instructional behaviors by other teachers show fewer or no systematic gains in student learning?

It was largely because of the work of the behaviorists and other experimental psychologists that researchers phrased the question in this way. Advances in research design and data analysis permitted them to look directly into classrooms for an answer. Moreover, federal policy makers indicated a strong interest in funding this research. If the researchers could show that what goes on in schools does indeed account for some of the variance in student achievement, the government's past investment in education would be vindicated and future investment continued.

At first, the research programs yielded little new understanding. But gradually, findings began to emerge showing that teachers do make a difference (one of the key books at the time was titled *Teachers Make a Difference*[11]) and that what happens in schools does account for a portion of the variance in student achievement. Despite continuing progress in this form of research, however, no one, to the best of our knowledge, has succeeded in showing that what teachers and schools do ever accounts, on average, for more than 15 percent, or at most 20 percent, of the variance in achievement. Still, that is no mean feat. Time in school does not consume more than 20 percent of the waking life of the student, so if what happens in school could be shown to account for as much as 20 percent of the variance in student achievement, that would be a fine record of accomplishment. (Note that these percentage figures are averages, determined by aggregating large populations of students. It may easily be the case that for any particular student, schooling can have a huge impact on that student's achievement, or virtually no impact at all.)

Beginning in the mid-1980s, research on teaching turned away from this teacher-process–student-product model to studies that employ a more diverse array of research designs and methods to examine more complex conceptions of teaching, learning, and classrooms. Some of the more recent research examines all three of these at once, focusing on the interactions between teachers, students, and subject matter within the specific setting of the school classroom. The work of Walter Doyle provides a good example of this genre of research.

Doyle's interest is in the way teachers and students interact to define the nature of the work that students do. He contends that while "teachers affect what students learn by describing specifications for assignments, providing explanations about the processes that can be used to accomplish work, serving as a resource while students are working, and managing accountability for products," the essential element of teaching is "the way teachers define and structure the work students are to do."[12] Doyle looks at the curriculum in classrooms as a "bundle of tasks," which teachers both structure and enact. In so doing, the teacher converts the official curriculum into a series of concrete events. The challenge for the teacher is to convert or translate curriculum in ways that generate tasks that are educative for the students. Given that so many tasks are designed to simply occupy students' time or manage their conduct in workgroups, the design and enactment of educative tasks is not a simple undertaking for the teacher.

Although different from the studies of instructional time, and definitely outside the category of process-product research, Doyle's work may still be thought of as contributing to the executive approach to teaching, particularly to the improvement of methods (*M*). As in the case of the instructional-time studies, the study of academic-task structures advances our understanding of how teachers and students engage in classroom events and activities that are either educative or noneducative. Doyle, like Berliner, is interested in assisting teachers in becoming more effective and productive. Doyle's work, however, rests on the view that what happens in classrooms is more a matter of the interactive dynamic among students, teachers, and subject matter, and less a matter of the teacher's simply assuming authority for directing and controlling events in the classroom. Thus in some ways, Doyle has brought some attention to the element of relationship (*R*) between teacher and student to the executive approach. Even so, the *R* element remains a recessive feature of the executive approach.

The Complexity of Modern Schooling

The executive approach to teaching is a powerful one. No other set of instructional methods can lay claim to accounting for so much (relatively speaking) of the variance in student achievement. But consider this: Suppose we took teaching out of the typical school classroom and placed it in a tutorial setting. Suppose there are only two or three students to one teacher. And suppose, further, that these few students know why they are studying with this teacher and willingly choose to be part of an educational relationship. Do you think the executive approach to teaching would be of much value in this setting? It would seem that the skills of time management, making provision for opportunity to learn, carefully aligning instruments of assessment with the actual curriculum, and other aspects of the executive approach are not nearly so salient in this new setting.

Why? Because there is very little that requires organizing or managing. The teacher is free to concentrate specifically on the students and on what they are learning. What does this perspective tell you about the executive approach? Take a moment to think about it. Let us see if your answer is the same as ours.

If the executive approach is far less compelling in a tutorial setting, yet seemingly necessary in a typical school classroom, then this approach to teaching may have much more to do with how we organize education in schools and how we engage learners in this form of education than it does with any root notion of what education is all about. To put it another way, the executive approach to teaching accounts for variance in achievement not because it has been shown to be a particularly good way to educate human beings, but because it works well in rooms of 600 square feet that are filled with twenty-five young people, many of whom, if given a choice, might choose to be somewhere else.

The executive approach to teaching seems to work because it fits so well the modern circumstances of teaching (review the vignette of Jim Barnes on page 1 for an example of this fit). If the circumstances were changed, the executive approach might be far less powerful. The power of this approach stems from its connection to the structure of modern-day schooling: to classrooms with fifteen to thirty-five students; to strong systems of accountability that make regular use of standardized tests; to a complex organizational structure consisting of differentiated ability groups, grade levels, and types of schools; to teachers who are variously licensed to work with some children but not others and with some subjects but not others. The No Child Left Behind Act, passed in 2002, with its hundreds of pages of regulations, standards, and mandates and with its sharp focus on knowledge outcomes for all students, further increases the complexity of American public schooling, thereby boosting the perceived value of the executive approach.

Perhaps it is necessary to adopt such an approach to teaching that capitalizes so well on the structural and organizational features of contemporary schooling, even though doing so may leave unaddressed many of the most desired ends (*E*) of education. Phrasing the point in this way suggests that there may be a conflict between managing a classroom as any good executive would manage a complex organization and, at the same time, pursuing and attaining the ideals involved in producing a fully educated human being. Quite a few scholars have argued that this is indeed the case, that the executive approach to teaching is alien to the pursuit of many of the more noble ends of education. They also argue that pursuing knowledge as an end in itself has some frightening downside consequences. We will examine these consequences in some detail in chapter 5. Right now, we turn our attention to an approach to teaching that differs dramatically from the executive approach. In this second approach, discussed in the chapter that follows, the student as a person has far more standing than the knowledge that is contained in the school curriculum. And methods, such as they are, have as much to do with valuing the knowledge the student already possesses as with imparting new knowledge.

Before you begin chapter 3, however, we urge you to examine the relevant cases and disputes in chapter 7. If you take a few moments to work through those that bear on the executive approach, as indicated in table 2 of chapter 7, you will not only have a better idea of this approach but also be better prepared to venture into an examination of the facilitator approach to teaching.

Chapter 3

The Facilitator Approach

The teacher as facilitator places a great deal of emphasis on students as persons. She is a facilitator in the sense that she encourages and nurtures the growth of students. Her students are her primary concern. As such, the facilitator does not elevate mastery of subject-matter knowledge to the most prominent position in the roster of educational outcomes. The teacher as facilitator values subject-matter knowledge, but less for its own sake and more for the contributions it makes to the growth of her students.

The facilitative teacher believes that his students arrive at the school-house door already in possession of a great deal of knowledge and understanding. This knowledge and understanding may not be the same as that contained in the formal school curriculum, but because they are acquired through the experience of living, they are very real for those children and vital to the youngsters' ability to function well in the home, neighborhood, and peer culture. One of the key tasks of the teacher is to facilitate the coming together of the world that a child brings to school with the world the school seeks to open to the child.

In order to accomplish this blending of two worlds, the facilitative teacher shows considerable regard for who his students are: their histories, their experiences, their needs and wants, their fears and interests, their strengths and shortcomings. On the MAKER framework, awareness of one's students (*A*) is central to the facilitator. Relationships (*R*), and Ends (*E*), also hold prominent positions, but both of these are tightly bound to awareness of the student as a person. Remember Nancy Kwong, the English teacher? (See the beginning of chapter 1.) She allows her students to choose the books they want to read and has them keep a journal so they can reflect on how they felt about what they read and who they were becoming. One readily infers that she is committed to a facilitator approach, given her concern for her students appears to take precedence over other variables in the instructional process. Do you agree? Is Kwong a facilitator? To answer with assurance, we must probe more deeply into the facilitator approach.

Your Middle School English Class

Imagine that you are hired to teach English to middle school children (say, grade eight). Some weeks before school begins, you start seriously preparing for the first weeks of school. What thoughts run through your head as you sit with tablet, textbooks, and other class materials in front of you? Are you thinking about how you will assist your students with their language proficiency in grammar, spelling, and writing? The assigned textbook appears to do a good job of covering these aspects of the curriculum, although perhaps you are considering expanding some sections and shortening others.

How about literature? How will you balance linguistic and literary considerations over the course of the year? As you ponder these questions, you are probably thinking about the students—wondering about the best way to elicit their interest in what you plan to teach. But who are these students you have in mind? Do they have names? Do you know anything about them? What do they care about, and what is their interest, if any, in the study of English? Here is a sneak preview of your eighth-grade English class—the one you will not see for four more weeks. The characteristics or conditions of the learners are indicated, and the number of students who share each condition is shown. Please read the list with some care, as we raise a few questions about it in the following paragraph.

Parents separated within the year	1
Parents divorced	4
Recently arrived from another country	3
Detests English grammar	5
Physically abused by one or both parents	2
Visited more than three foreign countries	2
Traveled through at least four U.S. states	15
Never traveled beyond seventy-five miles of home	7
Has recurring nightmares; gets little sleep	1
Loves sports and hip-hop artists	6
Family income below the poverty line	3
Enjoys building things	6
Takes Ritalin for hyperactivity disorder	3
Responds well to freedom and responsibility	8
Responds well to structure and authority	8
Feels very discouraged by lack of friendships	4

As you read through this list, did you wonder what these characteristics had to do with your teaching? Will they make a difference to the way you teach your class? Think about these questions for a moment. How will your teaching of English be different as a result of having six students who enjoy building things, or three who take Ritalin to control attention deficit hyperactivity disorder, or seven who have never ventured more than seventy-five miles from home? The executive teacher is likely to respond that these characteristics offer interesting background information, but do not fundamentally alter the way she is going to teach her classes. The facilitative teacher takes a very different position. If he is to honor and respect his students as persons, this knowledge of how they differ is essential to his planning and carrying out the activities of teaching. It will affect the way teacher and students talk to each other, what they talk about, and how the teacher plans to engage each student in the topics of instruction. It will also affect how the teacher responds to the character and quality of work each student produces in response to assignments. An extended quotation from a ninth-grade teacher reveals how important the lives of students are to the facilitative teacher:

> I teach writing to two very different groups of students. The first group might be described as a heterogeneously representative sample of ninth graders from our affluent suburb. The students in the Alternative High School program, on the other hand, are harder to describe. These students have for all intents and purposes "quit" school. They have stopped attending class on a regular basis and probably have not paid attention in class for many years. Their lives are rich in turmoil and trouble. Their parents can in almost every case be best described as dysfunctional, by which I mean that something has gone terribly awry in their parenting. The students physically abuse one another and their peers, and suffer abuse at the hands of others as a matter of course. Many are in trouble with the law, or have been at one time or another. They suffer an intense lack of self-esteem. When I began teaching them, it became clear to me that they could not succeed in an academic setting unless this lack of self-esteem was addressed in some way. I have tackled this primarily through writing.
>
> I tell all my students that writing is important because it comes directly from inside them. I believe that writing comes from a union of the mind and soul, and that it is the most personal thing students are asked to do in school. Consequently, when I ask students to write, I feel a strong obligation to be supportive of them and to encourage and praise them for their efforts as unique individuals. I ask both groups of my students to write about what they care about, what they know about—what they are experts in.
>
> As the students in the Alternative High School have begun to abandon their notions of "academic" writing, and reached into their own experiences and feelings for their material, they have begun to succeed in a way that they never believed they could. When Mark moved from writing a maximum of two sentences a day to writing a four-page piece

about his deer-hunting trip and the kill he made, we both succeeded. He had made a leap into believing that something that he knew and felt could be worthwhile for another person to read about; his self-esteem soared. His sense that he was interesting and capable and worthwhile translated directly into the attitude he brought to his other schoolwork, and he began to excel academically in a way that he had not since the second grade (he is eighteen years old now). The patience and encouragement with which I responded to his first tentative efforts at writing something that mattered to him paid off for me as a teacher. Not only did he begin to succeed in a much more traditional way as a student— he began to feel his worth as a human being.

This connection between writing and self-esteem is a very powerful one. By giving students constant positive feedback, I can help their confidence to soar. And when their confidence is high, they can achieve far more than if they feel ignorant and stupid and incapable. Because writing about what we know and care about is such an intimately personal act, it can only succeed in an atmosphere that respects the individual and nurtures that which is unique in each person. A logical outcome of a nurturing environment in which respect for personhood is paramount is that both good writing and self-esteem flourish.[1]

This excerpt from a teacher's diary offers a remarkably clear view of the facilitator approach. It illustrates not only the teacher's interest in and concern for the lives of students, but also the way the students' life experiences are brought into the subject matter of instruction. Notice that facilitation entails not simply becoming aware of the personal histories of one's students, but also helping them use the knowledge and understanding they bring to school. Part of what it means to respect the student as a person is to respect what that student has already learned about the world that shapes his or her everyday life.

The facilitator approach has a fascinating history, one that clearly shows why the *person* is so central to this approach. A look at the recent past of this approach also makes clear how ends (*E*) of a certain kind are integral to the facilitator approach. What the facilitative teacher is attempting to nurture is authenticity—helping every student become what he or she authentically is as a person and fellow human being. As you follow this recent history, you will gain a deeper sense of what the facilitator means by *authenticity*.

Historical Background

In the previous chapter, we mentioned President Johnson's Great Society programs and the Coleman Report. Just before that era, during the 1950s and into the early 1960s, education in the United States was making its closing arguments in the great educational debate of the preceding four decades. That debate was between traditional and progressive education. Traditional education emphasized learning subject matter, typically with strict discipline and little variation in the form and function of schooling. Progressive education sought to redress the heavy emphasis on mastering the traditional curriculum by devoting greater attention to the needs and interests of the students, as well as to the life circumstances that formed their present and possible future.

As educational institutions sought an accommodation to progressive educational ideals, the Soviet Union launched the first satellite to be placed in earth orbit, Sputnik. That the Soviet Union could precede the United States in outer space infuriated many American leaders, leading them to argue that the nation's schools must be improved if we were to remain competitive with then Communist Russia (the term *Russia* was often used to signify what at the time was the entire Soviet Union). The reform most often advocated by these leaders was an end to progressive education and a return to more traditional forms of schooling.

In the midst of this reaction against progressive education, President John F. Kennedy was assassinated (six years after the launch of Sputnik). His successor, Johnson, advocated strongly for pursuing both the war in Vietnam and massive federal programs of social justice. Many of the social justice initiatives proposed by his administration were occasioned by the celebrated 1954 *Brown v. Board of Education* decision, the U. S. Supreme Court case that overturned laws permitting the racial segregation of America's schools. The Johnson administration's support for social justice initiatives diverted mainstream attention from the traditional-versus-progressive debate. Meanwhile, the counterculture of the 1960s refashioned notions of progressive education into new theories and ideas. Humanistic education was perhaps the most dynamic and compelling of these new theories.

Humanistic education represents a fascinating conjunction of contemporary social criticism and a new version of psychology that was developed in opposition to behaviorism and experimental methods. Looking first at the social criticism of the time, it is possible to see why a new version of psychology would gain favor. Paul Goodman was one of the harshest and most read of the social critics. His book *Growing Up Absurd* had the force of holy writ for the sixties' counterculture.[2] In another book, *Compulsory Mis-Education*,[3] and in many articles written for magazines and journals, Goodman made a direct and powerful attack on school practices that were now nearly universal in the United States. Writing for the *Saturday Review* in 1968, he strongly endorsed the view that we can "educate the young entirely in terms of their free choice, with no processing whatever. Nothing can be efficiently learned, or, indeed, learned at all . . . unless it meets need, desire, curiosity, or fantasy."[4]

In what appears to be a direct swipe at the executive approach, Goodman argued, "It seems stupid to decide *a priori* what the young ought to know and then try to motivate them, instead of letting the initiative come from them and putting information and relevant equipment at their service."[5] The typical rejoinder to this contention was to point out that this way of educating the young may not be in the best interests of society in the long run. To which Goodman replied:

> If the young, as they mature, can follow their bent and choose their topics, times, and teachers, and if teachers teach what they themselves consider important—which is all they can skillfully teach anyway—the needs of society will be adequately met; there will be more lively, independent, and inventive people; and in the fairly short run there will be a more sensible and efficient society.[6]

At the time, this proposal was considered radical; it still is. Notice that Goodman gives a central role to choice for the learner. The learner chooses the content to be learned, when and how it is to be learned, and who is to teach it. The teacher's obligation in this setting is to enhance the learner's power to choose and to help the student use what is learned as an opportunity for personal growth. One of the most dramatic examples embodying this approach to teaching and learning is Summerhill, a British school founded by A. S. Neill some eighty years ago. Neill's book, *Summerhill: A Radical Approach to Child Rearing*,[7] describes this fascinating exemplar of student-dominated, choice-based schooling. A recent article in the *Phi Delta Kappan* magazine indicates that Summerhill continues to serve as a model for student-driven learning.[8]

The humanistic education advocated by Goodman, Neill, and other radical writers of the 1960s, such as George Dennison, Ivan Illich, Herbert Kohl, and Jonathan Kozol, is often linked to a psychology of learning that was in marked contrast to the two dominant schools of psychology at the time, functionalism and behaviorism. (Kohl and Kozol, by the way, continue in the early years of the twenty-first century to publish powerful critiques of contemporary schooling.) We turn now to consider this new psychology of learning.

Humanistic Psychology

Many of the educational ideas coming from social critics of the time found fertile expression in an alternative psychology known as humanistic, or "third-force," psychology. Gordon Allport, Abraham Maslow, and Carl Rogers were among the leading figures in this school of psychology. Each of these psychologists stresses the uniqueness of individuals and the difficulties that psychology, in its attempts to become a science of mind or behavior, has had in treating individual persons with proper regard for their unique properties.

Maslow, for example, does not deny the behaviorist contention that individuals act in response to stimuli, but he argues that this action must be understood as the result of an interaction between the person's needs and the unique "lifespace" of every person. Each one of us has a hierarchy of drives, from basic survival needs for food and water to such higher-level needs as to give and receive love, develop self-esteem, and appreciate beauty. A person who meets his or her needs to the highest level possible for his or her lifespace is, according to Maslow, a self-actualized person. A fully self-actualized person is one who possesses a balanced and integrated personality, with such positive traits as autonomy, creativeness, independence, altruism, and a healthy goal-directedness.[9] Although many educators embraced his notion of self-actualization, Maslow did not develop its implications for education. It is to the work of Carl Rogers that we must turn for the pedagogical implications of humanistic psychology.

"Teaching," claims Rogers, "is a vastly over-rated function."[10] It is most unfortunate that educators and the public think about, and focus on, teaching. It leads them into a host of questions which are either irrelevant or absurd so far as real education is concerned."[11] He bases this view of teaching on the importance of what he calls "experiential learning." This is learning that is filled with personal involvement; the whole person is in the learning event, rather than being a passive absorber of whatever the teacher dispenses. It is learning that is self-initiated. It is pervasive; it influences every aspect of the learner's being. It is evaluated by the learner, not by the teacher or by tests. It is rooted in meaning, which is to say that the learning has personal meaning for the learner; it advances the learner's power to understand and influence events that are important in his or her life.

Learning of this kind cannot be controlled by a teacher. It must be freely engaged in by the learner (a point that was made again and again by advocates for Summerhill-type schools). The teacher can only guide, suggest, encourage, and maybe even, when the occasion is appropriate, warn. Rogers believes that "anything that can be taught to another is relatively inconsequential and has little or no significant influence on behavior."[12] What is important is not what can be taught, but rather what is learned. The teacher is not one who imparts knowledge and skill to another, but one who helps another gain his or her own knowledge and skill. In the role of guide or facilitator, the teacher must be "a real person in his relationship with his students. He can be enthusiastic, he can be bored, he can be interested in students, he can be angry, he can be sensitive and sympathetic.

Because he accepts these feelings as his own he has no need to impose them on his students"[13]

Humanistic psychology, as Maslow and Rogers make quite evident, is a psychology based on freedom, choice, personal growth, and the development of emotional and mental health. In their view, education makes a significant contribution to these ends, but not by the traditional mechanisms of packaging subject-matter content for delivery to student learners. Instead, the student must be helped to attain his or her own actualization. The teacher's task is to direct the learner inward, toward the self, so that the learner is thereby enabled to reach outward, choosing the content to be acquired and the actions that follow from mastery of this content.

Normative Considerations

Humanistic psychologists incorporated into their psychology something that most academics and psychologists seek to get rid of. It is called "normativity." The closest everyday word for this more technical term might be *values*, but there are so many different meanings connected to the word *values* that we will be on much less contested ground if we stay with the word *normativity*. Normative considerations have to do with what *should* or *ought* to be the case, rather than with what is believed to be the case (descriptive considerations). Normative considerations often point to ideals and aims, to what we believe is best and right in the human species.

As you probably inferred from the discussion of the humanistic psychologists, they took a normative position with respect to persons. That is, they argued that children *should* learn in a particular way *if* they are to are to attain ends proper to being persons. In the case of the humanistic psychologists, these ends are about realizing our potential and doing so in ways that are authentic. These psychologists did not say, "This is how all children learn," which would be a descriptive account of learning (the type much favored by scientific psychology). Rather, they argued normatively, by advancing a set of proper ends for persons and then making the empirical claim these ends were best attained by certain kinds of teaching and learning. It was, in part, the normative character of humanistic psychology that led to its nickname, "third-force psychology."

We did not have occasion to discuss normativity in the executive approach. The reason is that there is not much of it there. Normativity is what brings ends, the *E* in MAKER, to the fore. When *E* is prominent in an approach, it signifies that the approach is rooted in certain ideals and aims, that the approach contains normative considerations. *E* plays a dominant role in the facilitator and liberationist approaches, but not in the executive approach. The reasons for this are worth considering.

Recall that in the executive approach, *M* and *K* are dominant elements. *E* does not occupy a position of importance, because, for the executive, *E* is so closely associated with *K*. That is, what the executive seeks is to have the students acquire the knowledge that is being taught, in the belief that possession of this knowledge is essential to such goals as a productive workforce, good citizenship, national security, and global competitiveness. Here you might want to interrupt the analysis to ask why we are not treating these goals as ends.

Good question. The answer is that the goals of the executive approach have a quite different form and character from those of the facilitator and liberationist approaches. The executive typically holds goals for schooling that are broadly societal and economic, and thus instrumental in character. For example, students should learn science, math, and English because these will lead to such outcomes as a productive workforce, global competitiveness, and so forth. The executive does not strive directly for such goals. Indeed, it takes more than good schooling to gain a productive workforce (jobs, monetary policy, and markets are a few of the other necessities). In contrast, the normative ends sought by the facilitator and liberationist are pursued directly with each student and grounded in a conception of what makes the student the best possible person.

In the course of the discussion of ends (*E*) in chapter 1, a distinction was drawn between ends, goals, and consequences. It was noted that in this book, the term *Ends* is reserved for the "grand and noble ideals that we seek for the children and youth who attend the nation's schools." Ideals of this kind are not much in evidence in the executive approach, save by inference (that is, if students master the subjects they are taught, then they will be happy, productive, and successful). Rather, such ends as there are in the executive approach are more like the goals of schooling rather than the ends that we as educators seek for each human being under our care. With this distinction in mind, let us return to the normative features of the facilitator approach.

Existential Roots

To the teacher as facilitator, the student's authenticity is not cultivated by acquiring remote knowledge that is unrelated to the quest for personal meaning and identity. Filling students' heads with knowledge that has been selected, packaged, and conveyed by others only keeps students from grasping themselves as human beings. It separates them from themselves by forcing them to attend, not to their own feelings, thoughts, and ideas, but to the sterile thoughts, images, and attitudes of others. The basic ideas that sustain so much of the normative stance in facilitative teaching can be found in a school of philosophy known as existentialism. It would take us far afield to explore existentialism in any depth, but we can touch on just enough to illustrate how it serves as a foundation for much of the facilitator approach to teaching.

One of the few tenets that existentialists such as Camus, Kirkegaard, and Dostoyevsky hold in common is that existence precedes essence, that we simply are before we are anything in particular. One of the best-known existentialists, Jean-Paul Sartre, explains:

> What do we mean by saying that existence precedes essence? We mean that man first of all exists, encounters himself, surges up in the world— and defines himself afterwards. If man as the existentialist sees him is not definable, it is because to begin with he is nothing. He will not be anything until later, and then he will be what he makes of himself. . . . Man is nothing else but that which he makes of himself. That is the first principle of existentialism.[14]

We define ourselves as we confront the world and choose our way through it. If we avoid these choices and their consequences, then we are, in fact, avoiding the essence of being human: our freedom. It was Sartre who wrote of persons fleeing from their freedom because absolute, total freedom is so frightening. It is scary to confront the view that we may do differently anything we are now doing, that we can always choose to act another way, think a different thought, feel a different emotion. Yet to be authentic, we must confront our freedom, we must create meaning for ourselves, and we must choose our way to and through our future.

The normativity that is characteristic of the facilitator approach helps us gain a better sense of how the *A* and the *E* of MAKER are interconnected. In order to achieve the ends called for, such as self-actualization, authenticity, and personal meaning, the teacher must have an awareness of her students. This awareness takes the form of insight into the life experiences of students as well as the knowledge and understanding that students bring with them as they pass through the schoolhouse door. To forge the critical links between *A* and *E*, the teacher has to attend to the quality of the relationship (*R*) with students. The *R* element assumes a quite special status in a modern version of facilitation known as *care pedagogy*.

Care Pedagogy

It is of more than passing interest to note that, despite the great personal appeal of humanistic education, it has not, since its heyday in the 1960s and 1970s, been very competitive with other approaches to teaching. Just as the philosophical school of existentialism never took root in American philosophy, humanistic psychology and humanistic education gained few long-term adherents among either social scientists or educators. There is, however, a quite modern variation that appears to be making some headway. It is often referred to as the pedagogy of care and is rooted in an ethical theory known as *care theory*.

In the early 1980s, as feminist thought gained a toehold in American culture, two books appeared that would do much to offer a foundation for this budding movement. The first was Carol Gilligan's *In a Different Voice* and the second was Nel Nodding's *Caring: A Feminine Approach to Ethics and Moral Education*.[15] In these two books, the authors argued for relational caring as the dominant ethic for the human species. While the expression "relational care" may strike some as soft and fuzzy, it is no such thing. It is proposed as an alternative to justice, the bedrock concept of ethics and jurisprudence in Western civilization since the time of Plato.

According to care theory, justice is an inadequate standard for human conduct. Justice, argue the care theorists, has permitted the moral rationale for such things as the egregious treatment of prisoners, acts of war, the slaughter of noncombatants, and indifference to poverty and disability. An ethic of care would prohibit such heinous acts, requiring instead that we do all in our power to enable others to grow and flourish. Sometimes care theorists use the same normative expressions as the earlier humanists, speaking of self-actualization and authentic selves.

In her recent work, Noddings offers a fairly succinct account of the caring relation. As you read her words, do not be put off by such terms as "motivational displacement." Instead, take the time to dig deeply into what she is saying here, as doing so will add more depth to your grasp of the facilitator approach.

> Attention—receptive attention—is an essential characteristic of the caring encounter. The carer, A, receives what-is-there in B. But clearly more than attention is required. A must respond in some way. If B is trying to accomplish something he may want A's help, or perhaps—as is often the case with children—B is simply calling out, "watch me, watch me." Thus, in addition to the attention that characterizes A's consciousness in caring, there is also a feature we might call *motivational displacement*. A's motive energy begins to flow toward B and his projects.[16]

Noddings then obliges us with an example, one quite pertinent to our topic:

> Ms. A, a math teacher, stands beside student B as he struggles to solve an equation. Ms. A can almost feel the pencil in her own hand. She anticipates what B will write, and she pushes mentally toward the next step, making

marks and erasures mentally. Her moves are directed by his. She may intervene occasionally but only to keep his plan alive, not to substitute her own. She introduces her own plan of attack only if his own fails entirely and he asks, "What should I do?" [17]

In this example, Noddings illustrates how motivational displacement follows from attention. To attend to another, in the context of care, is to have one's own motives displaced in favor of those of the one cared for. Among her examples: "If B is in pain, A will want to relieve that pain. If B needs to talk, A will listen. If B is perplexed, A will offer what she can to bring clarity to B's thinking." [18] The care theorist might be said to be grounding the normative ends of humanistic psychology in a robust theory of ethics. What changes here is the placement of R, the relationship.

Given the humanistic psychologists' low estimation of the value of teaching for learning, they gave little attention to the nature and quality of the relationship between teacher and student. The humanists appear to view the teacher more as a remover of barriers and impediments to choice, as a creator of environments of opportunity and possibility for the learner, than as one who forges profound relationships with students. Indeed the humanistic educators of the 1960s and 1970s might well regard the teacher's being so deeply engrossed in the learner as something of a danger to the learner's natural and free development.

Such differences recall the relationship, or lack thereof, between Jean-Jacques Rousseau's young student in *Emile* and his tutor. The tutor avoided interaction with Emile as much as possible, perceiving his role more as protecting Emile's natural development by ensuring his isolation from the evils of contemporary culture. While humanistic educators of the twentieth century might protest this eighteenth-century version of child rearing, they have more in common with Rousseau than they may care to admit. The care theorists, on the other hand, will roundly reject Rousseau's ideal of educating the young. To care is to be in relation to another. Indeed, so intensely in relation that the needs of the one being cared for become the abiding interest of the one who is caring.

Care pedagogy represents a fascinating evolution in humanistic education. While it is highly responsive to the social critiques of the 1960s and shares elements of humanistic psychology and existentialism, it stands quite independent of its precursors. It recasts the A so critical to the humanistic educators, into an R, such that A does not stand alone but as part of the R that obtains between the one caring and the cared for, between the teacher and the learner. Care pedagogy brings the teacher back into a much more crucial role in the growth of the learner than was the case in humanistic education.

This exploration of care pedagogy opens a line of inquiry that is highly pertinent to a set of complex and contentious issues in contemporary education. The set encompasses all topics, issues, and struggles that swirl about the terms *multiculturalism* and *diversity*. As the following section makes clear, the facilitator deals with this set differently from most of what you may have previously encountered when hearing about multiculturalism and diversity in the schools. In the context of facilitation, it is all about the formation of identity.

Facilitating Identity

The facilitator approach to teaching provides an exceptional opportunity to introduce an aspect of teaching that is much on the minds of today's educators. Most often identified as multiculturalism or diversity, it is the role of schooling in promoting an understanding of and respect for certain human differences. The most prominent of these differences in our time are race, ethnicity, gender, disability, and sexual orientation. These are subjects of considerable struggle and debate across the entire planet, and topics of considerable weight in the arenas of American politics, economy, and social life.

Among the questions repeatedly raised on these subjects are the following: Is race or ethnicity an actual barrier to equal opportunity in America? If so, what are the best ways to eradicate these barriers? Can one prize one's status as a member of a minority group and simultaneously prize being an American? Should children with severe disabilities share the same classrooms as their able-bodied classmates? Should same-sex relationships be given the same legal standing as heterosexual relationships? The same social standing? Is it proper for government to intervene in the educational and vocational sectors in order to affirmatively assist persons who have previously been ill treated by virtue of race, ethnicity, gender, disability, or sexual orientation? Are schools proper and appropriate sites for addressing these great human struggles, and if so, how should they go about doing so?

Any reader of the editorial and opinion pages of today's newspapers knows how very contentious these topics are. Indeed, discussions on these topics and the controversy that they engender are part of the fabric of everyday life in the United States and many other nations. Because they are so contentious, it is a challenge to present them in a way that unequivocally demonstrates their educational importance. The facilitator approach opens a path for doing so.

When the facilitator claims that among his ends are authenticity, growth, and self-actualization, he is saying that it is essential to address certain questions. Among them are, Who am I? To what do I belong? What are my roots? How am I recognized by others? What is it that I am becoming? These are questions of identity. They are questions about how the self is being formed and coming to be understood. The facilitator believes that these questions are as much a part of the educational process as binomial equations, predicate nominatives, and the signing of the Magna Carta.

Granting the facilitator's point for the moment—that these identity questions are vital to the educative process—we can then inquire about the components or building blocks of identity. What is it that goes into the formation of our identities? The answer is, it depends. It depends on where and to whom we are born; on where we are reared; on friends, neighborhoods, and associations that make up our life experiences; on the stories we are told and the songs we learn to sing; and on how we are recognized and treated by others, particularly when these others are more powerful or more privileged than we are.

An enormously powerful influence on identity formation is exerted when a person comes to understand that he or she is different from some norm or standard, some seemingly settled and valued way to be that the person seems unable to have access to or claim. The person begins to grasp not only that he or she is different, but that he or she also is less valued because of this difference. This realization has the potential to seriously impair the healthy formation of identity—identity characterized by growth, authenticity, and self-realization.

Among the ways of coping with the recognition that one is different and somehow less valued because of this difference is to unite with others who share this difference, seeking honor in and celebration of the difference. One does this not only to diminish some of the harmful social and economic consequences of being different from the dominant or majority group, but also to change the way the majority group recognizes those who are different. These efforts to celebrate one's difference and to alter the way this difference is recognized account for many of the features of multicultural or diversity programs that are pursued in school contexts. The intent of such programs is to aid in the formation of a strong, positive identity. This objective is highly consistent with the ends espoused by the facilitator.

As we shall see in the following chapter, however, an interest in multiculturalism and diversity is not the sole province of the facilitative teacher. The liberationist approach, particularly in its emancipationist form, is also concerned with how differences in such things as race, culture, and gender are dealt with in the context of the school. What distinguishes the facilitator from the liberationist is the facilitator's focus on the person—in the form of both awareness (A) and relationship (R)—to achieve an authentic, self-actualized human being (the liberationist, as we will see, depends more on E and K in the formation of identity). For the facilitator, the pursuit of diversity and cultural sensitivity is not so much about politics, ideology, or social justice as it is about doing what is best to aid in the formation of a fully capable, fully functioning person, one who is self-aware and able to make thoughtful choices.

If we have succeeded in explaining this connection between identity and facilitation, it will be apparent why the facilitator not only acknowledges (read "does not hide from or ignore") important differences between his students, but also attends carefully to the various ways students recognize one another. To observe teachers skilled at acknowledgment and recognition of important human differences is to behold an awesome, inspiring performance. Such teachers' relationships to their students are deeply embedded in knowing the students and caring for them; they establish clear expectations for classroom interactions and commend actions in accordance with these expectations, they censure improper or unkind recognition with directness and compassion, they find and publicly praise what is special and worthy in the important differences that characterize students, and they exemplify in their own conduct the principles and practices they seek from their students.

There is more to be said about multiculturalism and diversity in later chapters. Our intent at this point has been to show how these elements can be viewed as an almost natural aspect of the facilitator approach. We are also trying to set the stage for showing how a commitment to multiculturalism and diversity can manifest itself differently depending on which approach to teaching one takes. For the remainder of this chapter, we take up two prominent, important ideas that are frequently associated with teaching as facilitation: constructivism and multiple intelligences.

Constructivism

Constructivism and multiple intelligences are two quite different notions about how we learn, but both are derived from the same school of psychology, known as cognitive psychology. As such, both notions attend to how the mind processes experience, particularly how mental organization, memory, and learning are accomplished. From an understanding of how the mind organizes, represents, and recalls information, we can draw inferences about how to organize instruction. These inferences permit us to assist the learner to acquire information in ways that are most closely aligned with how the mind processes information. The result, argues the cognitive psychologist, is that learning occurs with greater proficiency and effectiveness than would otherwise be the case. Constructivism provides a case in point.

Put simply, constructivism contends that children learn by constructing meaning for what they experience. It looks like a simple, even obvious, point, but it is actually quite complex. It means that learners do not simply "take in," in some pure form, that which is presented to them. Instead, they try to make sense of it, often by connecting it to other information or mental organizations already present. This process might alter the mental frameworks that the learner already possesses, or it might cause the student to amend the new information to fit the framework already in place. Jean Piaget, the renowned developmental psychologist, referred to these processes as *assimilation* and *accommodation*. One of the better-known examples he offers is of the child who does not yet possess the idea or framework of object permanency. A child lacking the notion of object permanency believes that an object disappears or ceases to exist when it is hidden from sight, as, for example, when the object is covered with a blanket. Lacking a framework to correctly assimilate what has happened before his or her eyes, the infant accommodates the experience to a framework that denies substance to objects that are out of sight.

Students at any level of development can make similar mistakes. They can take in information and "misfit" it into a faulty framework while trying to make sense of it. The constructivist teacher attempts to avoid this misrepresentation by assisting students to acquire concepts and mental structures that accommodate subject matter in ways that are both valid and meaningful. The constructivist encourages students to use whatever experience, knowledge, and mental frameworks they bring to school, while guiding them in the formulation of newer, more powerful frameworks and concepts in order to assimilate and accommodate the subject matter of study.

Given that the assimilations and accommodations take place in the student's mind, they are not visible to the teacher. Thus it is not always evident to the teacher when the student, like the infant, is making an invalid assimilation or accommodation. For example, two students can give the right answer on a test, but only one of them is processing information with a valid framework. The student using the invalid framework happened to obtain the right answer on this particular question, but this same framework will yield incorrect answers on related questions while the valid framework will produce correct answers to the related questions. The positive side of constructivism is that it allows for and attends carefully to the connections between the mental "maps" the students have when they enter the classroom and the knowledge and understanding the teacher seeks to present once they are there. The downside of constructivism is that students may believe that they correctly understand new material when in fact they do not, and the teacher may conclude that their understanding is correct when it is not.

While this downside is of concern to constructivists, they argue that it is simply a given in the learning process, that it happens in any event, and thus that it must be accounted for. If a certain level of accuracy or validity is essential, argue the constructivist educators, then it must be obtained by careful acknowledgment of the meaning-making initiatives of the student. Indeed, you may hear some constructivists argue that there are no right answers, only the answers that students give as a result of the diligent application of their mental powers.

The "there are no correct answers" advocates typically stir a great deal of controversy, especially among those holding traditional and more conservative views of education. Those who advocate for treating any authentic answer as a correct answer do not deny that information can be presented to children in ways that keep it "pure" and permit a right-answer strategy to learning. But consider the cost. The learner likely creates some mental space in which to store this information, a space that is purposefully walled off from other information in the mind. The information is then held until the time of the test, when it is "dumped" out and promptly forgotten. A humorous analogy is that it is like having a pizza delivered, but instead of eating it, we freeze it for a period of time then ship it back to the vendor. That doesn't make much sense, does it?

No, it certainly does not, the constructivist would say. New information, new experience, new stimuli—all must be offered in ways that *facilitate* the learner's imparting meaning to it, typically by connecting it to understandings already held and building new frameworks to accommodate it. To prevent such meaning-making is to wall off the new information, risking the learner's disinterest in it and its complete loss once it has been recalled for test or recitation. Speaking of the learner's disinterest in what is presented in school, another view of how children learn suggests that good education involves far more than presenting the usual subjects in the school curriculum.

Multiple Intelligences

When we refer to another person as being smart or intelligent, what are we saying about that individual? Typically we are commending his or her ability to acquire and retain a large amount of important information and ponder this information critically and creatively. In so doing, we are, according to Howard Gardner—the developer of the theory of multiple intelligences—picking out just one or two kinds of intelligence and ignoring several others. Gardner argues that human beings have the ability to solve many different kinds of problems and make or create things that are valued in one or more cultural settings.

In his 1983 work, *Frames of Mind*,[19] Gardner argued for seven intelligences:

Linguistic intelligence (as possessed by a poet, for example)
Logical-mathematical intelligence (as in a physicist or mathematician)

Spatial intelligence (sculptor or architect)
Musical intelligence (cellist or conductor)
Bodily-kinesthetic intelligence (dancer, athlete)
Interpersonal intelligence (sensitivity to others; for example, a teacher)
Intrapersonal intelligence (possessing a well-developed sense of self)

In a later work, *Intelligence Reframed*,[20] Gardner suggests two additional forms: naturalist intelligence, which is the ability to recognize and categorize objects in nature; and existential intelligence, which is a capacity to grapple with the profound questions of human existence. These additions have not yet had much discussion in or application to school settings, so it is more common to refer to the seven intelligences.

Have we presented enough of the theory for you to make an informed guess as to why it might appeal to the facilitative teacher? If you go back to the *A* in MAKER, you will note that Gardner's theory of seven intelligences offers a fascinating way to become more aware of one's students. So often we think of intelligence as only verbal or logical-mathematical, and thus we fail to pay equal regard to the other capabilities of the student. The notion that intelligence extends well beyond the verbal and logical-mathematical provides the facilitative teacher with another way to gain a better understanding of his students and assist them in becoming authentic, self-actualized human beings.

Another aspect of MI (Multiple Intelligence) theory is that it supplies the facilitative teacher with educationally relevant reasons for respecting the choices that students make. Recall that choice is a key feature of the facilitative setting, yet it has not always been easy for teachers to honor student choices that appeared unrelated to their development of verbal and logical-mathematical abilities. The idea that there are other intelligences worthy of cultivation in the setting of the school offers the teacher a strong rationale for supporting a broad range of choices as students pursue their interests and talents.

A note of caution is in order here. MI theory does not support ignoring the development of one or more intelligences while pursuing the cultivation of some other intelligence. Indeed, Gardner contends that many, and in some cases all, the intelligences often work jointly. Accomplishments and achievements on the students' part typically call for the use of several different intelligences. Consider dance as an example. How many intelligences might be involved in a performance? Certainly spatial, musical, and bodily-kinesthetic are primary, yet it is relatively easy to imagine circumstances that call for several others.

Like all theories, MI has its critics. Constructivism does, too. If you would like to explore these criticisms while learning more about both these theories of learning, take a look at one of the companion volumes in the series of which this book is a part, the volume titled *Perspectives on Learning*.[21] Regardless of the criticisms, however, it is clear that both theories are easily situated within the facilitator approach. Both represent the student as an active agent in his or her own learning and call on the teacher to respect this agency. Both expand the teacher's capacity for becoming aware of her students, as well as for honoring the choices that students make.

Notions of expanding awareness of students and student choice, of authenticity and self-actualization, while central to the facilitator approach, recede in prominence in the third and final approach to teaching that we will consider, the liberationist approach. This approach returns K to a central position, but in a form different from that seen in the executive approach. In its doing so, the student as person occupies a different, perhaps less powerful, position than in the facilitator approach. Let's see how that works.

Chapter 4

The Liberationist Approach

While the names given to the first two approaches seem straightforward enough—we've all heard of executives and facilitators—the name given to the third approach is not part of many everyday vocabularies. Yet most of us have heard the terms *liberal education* and *liberal studies*. The liberationist approach is rooted in notions of liberal education, wherein the goal is to liberate the mind to wonder, to know and understand, to imagine and create, using the full intellectual inheritance of civilized life.

Origins of This Approach

Although there is some dispute about the origins of liberal education, it is generally presumed (at least among Western scholars) that it began with the ancient Greeks, particularly with the work of Plato and Aristotle. These two figures are credited with developing the idea of purposefully preparing the young to lead lives of high, noble purpose. While the idea may seem unexceptional to us now, consider the immense change it represented in its time. The notion that persons can use their minds to formulate ideals of human possibility and perfection and then pursue these ideals as a part of living was an extraordinary advance. It shifted the purpose of education from the cultivation of skills needed to hunt, gather, farm, or produce to the fostering of skills needed to think, deliberate, discern, imagine, and investigate.

Such skills, however, are best acquired from the subject matters of the various disciplines of human inquiry. For the liberationist, it is these subjects, properly framed and presented, that lead to the liberation of the mind, freeing it from the constraints imposed by ordinary, everyday experiences; from the chance circumstances of birth and environment; from the rigid categories imposed by traditions, norms, and taboos.

Just as the facilitator approach contained a variation (care pedagogy), so does the liberationist approach. This variation is a relative newcomer, especially in light of the "age" of the liberationist approach. We call it *emancipatory teaching*, although its advocates typically refer to it as "critical pedagogy."[1] Emancipatory teaching focuses on freeing the person to act in ways that exemplify high principles of human welfare. It thus modifies the liberationist approach with a decided orientation to social and political action. Before becoming too deeply involved in an explanation of this variation, we should gain a deeper sense of the main approach.

Features of the Liberationist Approach

If you turn back to the description of Roberto Umbras at the beginning of chapter 1, you will quickly gain a sense of the liberationist approach. For the liberationist, ends (*E*) and knowledge (*K*) are dominant, while method (*M*), awareness of the student (*A*), and relationship (*R*) play a reduced role. The liberationist, like the facilitator, teaches in order to realize certain ends for students. But unlike the facilitator, the liberationist is interested in how the intellectual inheritance of the human race is brought to bear in the formation and pursuit of these ends. That is, the ends of the liberationist are profoundly shaped by *K*, while those of the facilitator are not.

If, for example, a student decided that mastery of, say, history, was not worthy of her time or energy, the facilitator would be inclined to permit the student to make this choice (the facilitator might do so reluctantly but recall that student choice is one of the most powerful, determinative features of the facilitator approach). The liberationist, however, would not permit this choice, for a command of history is essential if one is to grasp and advance the intellectual achievements of the species. Unlike the facilitator, the liberationist has a conception of a worthy and capable person that is deeply connected to the great bodies of knowledge that humankind has painstakingly developed over the millennia. The liberationist contends that we are not free to dismiss these bodies of knowledge, for ultimately our capacity to understand our freedom and to choose wisely depend on our grasp of the full range of knowledge and understanding amassed by humankind.

Perhaps you are wondering how the classical liberationist differs from the executive, given that *K* plays a significant role in both approaches. The answer to this question is very important, indeed essential, to gaining a good grasp of the liberationist approach. Recall that for the executive, the acquisition of *K* is the end that the teacher pursues. Thus for the executive, *E* and *K* are virtually equivalent. But the liberationist does not pursue *K* as an end in itself, but rather seeks to initiate the student into the collected wisdom and understanding of the species. Consider these words by British educator and philosopher John Passmore:

> To be educated one must be able to participate in the great traditions of imaginative thought—science, history, literature, philosophy, technology—and to participate in these traditions one must first be instructed, must learn a discipline, must be initiated. . . . The critical spirit which a

teacher is interested in developing is a capacity to be a critical participant within a tradition.[2]

The liberationist does not seek persons who are only knowledgeable (as many atrocities have been committed by persons who possess extensive knowledge), but persons who are also just and loving, who are imaginative in thought and discerning in conduct, and who are committed to the advancement of humankind. For the liberationist, *E* is founded on grand, noble ideals. Harvard philosopher and educator Israel Scheffler captures well the ideals of the liberationist approach to teaching:

> The aims of education must encompass the formation of habits of judgment and the development of character, the elevation of standards, the facilitation of understanding, the development of taste and discrimination, the stimulation of curiosity and wonder, the fostering of style and a sense of beauty, the growth of a thirst for new ideas and visions of the yet unknown.[3]

Your High School Class

In an effort to translate these elegant ideals into practice, we again imagine you with your own classroom. You recently completed college with a double major in math and physics, plus a secondary-school teaching credential. You are very proud of that achievement and even prouder that you turned down several job offers in private industry because you want to be a teacher. You have long regretted what you regard as the poor preparation that secondary students receive in math and the natural sciences. You love these fields and look forward to sharing your knowledge with your students. You have your pick of schools; preparation like yours is not an everyday occurrence for beginning teachers. You select a fine high school in a middle-class, racially mixed suburban community.

You have five periods, two of physics and three of math. You prepare extensively for these courses, supplementing the textbooks with workbooks, your own supporting materials, and a full range of visual aids, including colorful charts and graphs, posters, slides, Web searches, and selected films or videos depicting famous scientists and mathematicians struggling with the great intellectual problems of their times. In each course, your aim is that as many students as possible will confront the material in the way that a physicist or mathematician might.

For example, for the general physics class you decide to begin the unit on electricity simply, using a "breadboard" to illustrate the flow of electrical energy in a flashlight and ordinary house lamp. Before the first period of that lesson is over, you plan to introduce the concepts of circuits, polarity, resistance, and current flow. In subsequent lessons, you will discuss the basic mathematics typically used in electrical computations, then move on to the atomic character of electrical energy. Along the way, you will introduce the students to Gilbert, Faraday, Maxwell, and Neumann. By the end of the unit, you hope to have covered conduction, resonance, filtration, and magnetic effects, as well as thermal and biochemical effects.

How do you plan to teach all this content? By using questions to interrogate the everyday notions that your students have about physical phenomena, encouraging them to find answers to these questions. By involving them in disciplined inquiry that promotes their asking their own questions and seeking answers to these questions. By carefully adding to their store of new knowledge and understanding, building upon these additions to promote ever deeper and more powerful questions. Your hope is to initiate your students, as Passmore alludes to above, into the grand traditions of human discovery and human knowledge.

To do this, you arrange for your students to move from hands-on experiments to theoretical abstractions and back again to hands-on work. Your own instruction varies from lecture-type presentations to laboratory demonstrations, from providing the most current understanding of the topic to giving perspective through historical accounts and biography, as well as connecting the topic to related material in other disciplines. For example, in the unit on sound, you develop the connections between the aesthetics of music and the physics of sound. In the unit on light, you link the physical properties of light with the art of the great masters.[4]

Your plans rest on far more than the students' simply mastering the prescribed content of the physics textbook. You are seeking to develop the content of physics so that students can engage it in ways that elicit wonder and curiosity, that cultivate a respect for evidence and a sense of truth, that prompt imagination and creativity, and that connect this field of inquiry to other fields of inquiry (this recalls the Scheffler quotation, with its the elegant phrasing, several paragraphs back). In order to accomplish these ends, you have to model and exemplify them as the teacher. When you do so, we speak of your possessing a manner of a certain kind.

Manner in Teaching

Manner is something every teacher has; indeed, it is something that all of us have. We often hear talk of liking another person's manner, or of wishing that someone presented a different manner when around others. Manner is a general way of acting and is usually associated with certain traits or dispositions, such as being gracious, fair-minded, stern, witty, mean, compassionate, angry, tolerant, pigheaded, or affectionate. Given these characteristics, the idea of manner is related to the similar-sounding notion of manners, but the latter is more restrictive in its range. When we speak of manners, we are typically referring to being polite and socially respectful toward others. Having good manners (or poor ones) is a part of our manner, but only a small part. In this book, manner should be understood as the way one's entire personality is made manifest in various contexts.

Learning to teach is in part taking on the manner of a teacher. There are, for instance, certain moral and intellectual characteristics that are vital to good teaching. Among them are the ability to listen attentively, to be fair and honest in one's dealings with the students in one's care, to be skeptical about claims for which there is little or no evidence, to show respect for differences between persons, and to provide criticism in ways that assist the student to improve without diminishing the desire to keep trying.

If manner is a crucial part of what is involved in teaching, why did we not mention it before? Because it has a special place in the liberationist approach, even though it may be an aspect of any approach to teaching. The liberationist approach *requires* the taking on of a particular manner as well as the ability to make that manner evident to one's students. Without a manner of a certain kind, the liberationist approach fails. The reasons are fairly obvious: You are, for example, far less likely to succeed in teaching critical thinking to your students if you are not a critical thinker and never exemplify critical thinking in your classroom (that is, if it is not part of your manner). We are not saying it cannot be done (some students will think critically no matter how naive their teachers are). We are saying that is far less likely to happen if you cannot do it yourself and do not understand what is involved in fostering this trait in others.

The manner of the teacher is essential to the liberationist approach, for it determines, in large measure, whether the knowledge and skill to be learned will free the mind or simply trap it with dull and irrelevant facts and skills. One of the foremost contemporary advocates for the liberationist approach, R. S. Peters, has illuminated the idea of manner in his discussion of what he calls "principles of procedure" for teaching such subjects as science or history:

> There must be respect for evidence and a ban on "cooking" or distorting it; there must be a willingness to admit that one is mistaken; there must be non-interference with people who wish to put forward objections; there must be a respect for people as a source of argument and an absence of personal invective and contempt for what they say because of who they are. To learn science is not just to learn facts and to understand theories; it is also to learn to participate in a public form of life governed by such principles of

procedure. Insofar, therefore, as a person is educated scientifically, he will have to absorb these principles of procedure by means of which the content of scientific thought has been accumulated and is criticized and developed.[5]

These principles of procedure are made evident in one's manner. The teacher must not only display this manner but also call attention to and encourage its imitation by students. It is not enough for the liberationist that knowledge and skills are simply acquired by students, no matter how fully or completely. They must be acquired in a manner appropriate to the kind of knowledge it is. Indeed, the initiation that the liberationist is attempting to accomplish can only be achieved by bringing the proper manner together with "the great human traditions of imaginative thought" (Passmore's words) in order to realize the noble ends of the liberationist approach.

The teacher's power to exhibit an appropriate manner and to foster it in his students is, to no small extent, determined by the nature of the content at his disposal. The richness and sophistication of the teacher's manner is tightly related to the richness and sophistication of the content. If the material to be learned is "dumbed down," if it is grossly simplified, reduced to such a basic level that there is no nuance, no complexity, no ambiguity, it is likely to offer a very poor opportunity for the display and encouragement of enlightened or sophisticated manner.

This last comment about manner is one of the more important reasons why great literature, great art, great music, and other greats are so essential to the liberationist curriculum. The "greats" possess the levels of complexity and nuance so important to the cultivation of critical discernment, imagination, and deep insight. Their range and depth call for a manner that is commensurate, allowing the teacher to model for the students a manner that manifests the highest standards of thought and action while also encouraging the students to follow along.

The concept of manner has been examined in some depth here because it is a critical feature of the liberationist approach. However, at the outset of this chapter we noted that K and E are the principal elements of the MAKER framework for the liberationist. Ends (E) have been under discussion since the beginning of this chapter, but knowledge (K) has not yet received the attention it deserves. It is to knowledge that we now turn.

The Element of Knowledge

Recall that K was a dominant element in the executive approach, and it appears again as a dominant element here in the liberationist approach. How can two such different approaches share the same element, as the differences are critical to understanding both approaches?

The *K* in the executive approach is, as pointed out earlier, highly specified. It is made up of discrete facts, ideas, topics, and domains, often expressed in the form of measurable outcomes. This kind of tight specifica-
tion is required if objective, standardized tests are used to determine what,
if anything, the students gained from instruction. Recall that the teacher's
task is to move *K* from its source to the mind of the learner. The methods of
instruction in the executive approach are powerfully influenced by practices that have been shown to produce such gains in student achievement.
The liberationist does not see *K* as discrete, specifiable somethings to be got
into the heads of students, but rather as a grand set of insights, understandings, ideas, theories, and procedures into which the student is to be
initiated.

For the liberationist, an end of education is for the student to take up
membership in civilized life, to join what Michael Oakeshott called "the
human conversation," to inherit what John Dewey referred to as "the funded capital of civilization." *K* is the symbol for these bodies of knowledge
and understanding that constitute the funded capital of civilization and
that prepare the young to participate in the human conversation.

The liberationist places some strict controls on what counts as knowledge and understanding, and thus on what is proper to the curriculum.
One of the most thorough contemporary explications of these controls has
been put forward by P. H. Hirst.[6] He argues that knowledge can be divided
into seven forms: mathematics, physical sciences, human sciences, history,
religion, literature and fine arts, and philosophy. Hirst states that these
seven forms cover all the kinds of things we as human beings can come to
know about in the world. The best education is the one that initiates students into these forms of knowledge.

Each form has its own special concepts that capture key aspects of
human experience. For example, to make sense of artistic experiences, we
need a concept of beauty; to make sense of experiences in the natural, physical world, we need such concepts as truth, fact, and evidence; and to understand mathematical phenomena, we need the concept of number.
Besides these key concepts, each form of knowledge, according to Hirst,
has a distinctive logical structure of its own (think of the difference, for example, between the rules for deducing proofs in mathematics and the rules
of grammar in a language), a set of special skills and methods for making
knowledge claims in that form (think of scientific method as an example),
and a set of unique standards for publicly testing and judging claims (literary or artistic criticism are examples). Thus, to acquire a discipline (physics,
chemistry, history, psychology, and so forth) is to learn its major ideas, understand its logical structure, be able to undertake controlled inquiry within its domain of experience, and know what determines the merit and
worth of one's findings or productions.

When these notions of the nature of knowledge are combined with the idea of manner, one begins to sense the profound difference between the *K* of the executive and the *K* of the liberationist. For the executive, *K* is presented to be acquired. For the liberationist, it is presented not only to be acquired but also for what it enables the person to do and to become. Both the executive and the liberationist would agree that children need to know math, history, literature, science, and the other subjects of the customary school curriculum. But for the executive, simply knowing these subjects appears to be sufficient. Not so for the liberationist. The liberationist views these subjects as vehicles for acquiring the capacity to reason well, to make good judgments, to discern aesthetic qualities, and to foster curiosity and wonder. What glorious ends these are, and how could there be any variation on them? We are about to find out.

Emancipatory Teaching

Emancipatory teaching is a variant of the liberationist approach, with a strong social and political orientation. It is aligned with the notion of *praxis*, a concept that forges strong links between ideas and action. The emancipationist argues that the purpose of education is not simply to initiate the young into the civilized, enlightened life, but to encourage and enable them to critique its shortcomings and to act to realize its promises.

In his foreword to a recent book on this subject, Henry Giroux, one of the best-known spokespersons for emancipatory teaching, offers the following defense for this form of teaching. Note how Giroux grounds his case on a critique of current society and an urgency for change.

> Public schooling in the United States is suffering from an identity crisis. Caught amid the call for testing, privatization, and choice, the legacy of schooling as a crucial public sphere has been subordinated to the morally insensitive dictates of market forces. . . . One result has been the rewriting of what schools are and might become. Lost from the new discourse of educational reform is any notion of social justice and democratic community. Reduced to the language of competitiveness and individual gain, it has become difficult to relate the mission and purpose of schooling to a public discourse that addresses racism, poverty, sexism, nihilism, widespread ignorance, and cultural despair.[7]

The emancipationist sees the social world as a place of constant struggle and oppression where those who have power, privilege, and status assert themselves and those who do not have power or privilege accept their diminished status and the fate that follows from it. The emancipationists argue that schools often serve as instruments of social reproduction in which the lower classes learn to be docile workers who follow orders and the upper classes are trained for leadership and the exercise of power. The end (E) of emancipationist teaching, then, is to free the minds of students from the unconscious grip of oppressive ideas about such things as their class, gender, race, or ethnic status. These ideas imprison and debilitate thought and action, cutting persons off from genuine opportunities for a better life. But one becomes free of these oppressive ideas not simply by recognizing them as oppressive, but by doing something about them. That is the meaning of praxis, wherein one's understanding of an idea is completed through action.

Perhaps the best-known early articulator of the role of the emancipationist teacher is Paulo Freire, the Brazilian educator who developed a method for teaching illiterate adult peasants in the northeastern region of Brazil. In 1964 he was exiled for his work. His book *Pedagogy of the Oppressed*[8] sets forth the political and philosophical basis for his educational ideas, as well as the pedagogical practices he developed to stimulate and sustain "critical consciousness" in people.

Freire's fundamental concern is the liberation of poor, powerless, unschooled people who have been subject to slavelike domination by the wealthy and the powerful. He believes that an oppressive view of social reality is imposed by the dominant groups on the oppressed, making it impossible for the latter to perceive and assess their situation or even to think it can be otherwise. This version of social reality is inculcated through words, images, customs, myths, and popular culture and in countless obvious and subtle ways that pervade public life. The oppressed accept this version as reality and are psychologically devastated by it. By accepting the dominant view, they come to think of themselves as inferior and helpless. They acquire the personality traits characteristic of oppressed people: fatalism, self-deprecation, and emotional dependence. (If you are familiar with the work of Karl Marx, you have probably noted the parallels between Freire and Marx. The emancipationists employ a good deal of Marxist theory to interpret and explain contemporary educational events.)

The primary task of education, for Freire, is to overcome these attitudes and replace them with traits of active freedom and human responsibility. This cannot be done by treating the oppressed as objects whose behaviors are to be transformed by the teacher. Rather, they must be treated as active human agents who deserve our help, so that they can achieve their own liberation. They need to be awakened "to see themselves as men engaged in the ontological and historical vocation of becoming more fully human."[9] This awakening is accomplished through dialogue. The task of the teacher as emancipator is problem posing—"posing of the problems of men in their relations with the world."[10] The students and their teacher must become collaborators, coinvestigators developing together their consciousness of reality and their images of a possible, better reality. This ability to step back from an unconscious acceptance of things as they are and to perceive the world critically, even in the midst of pervasive, powerful, subtle forces tending to distort and oppress, is what Freire means by attaining critical consciousness.

In the United States in more recent times, the work of Michael Apple, Henry Giroux, Peter McClaren, Stanley Aronowitz, Ira Shor, Barry Kanpol, and others[11] has carried forward the emancipationist stance against the evils of social reproduction. Translating emancipatory pedagogy into everyday teaching practice has been a challenge, however, partly because so much of the work on the subject is theoretical and interpretative rather than practical. Fortunately, an increasing number of efforts to bridge this gap have emerged, as seen in the work of Patricia Hinchey, Ira Shor, and Joan Wink.[12] These writers have sought to describe how teaching is conducted and how classrooms look when grounded in emancipatory principles.

What one gleans from these writings is the importance of focusing instruction on problems, such as war and peace, racial and economic injustice, and the search for sustainable environments. As student attention is directed to these problems, students are assisted in locating resources that expand their understanding of the ideas in, theories on, and research into the problems. The students are encouraged to engage in open, respectful dialogue with their classmates to explore other ways of thinking about the problems, as well as to gain the benefit of the work other students have done. As they gain in understanding, the students are directed to consider possible actions that would offer relief or resolution for the problems under study.

A very salient feature of emancipatory teaching is its attention to democratic ideals and civic responsibilities. A hallmark of the emancipationist is the consideration given to social justice, particularly as made manifest in discrimination grounded in social class, race, gender, and sexual orientation. We conclude this chapter with a brief look at both democracy and social justice.

Democratic Citizenship

The word *democracy* is much used but little understood. Roughly defined, it signifies rule by the people in contrast to rule by aristocrats, the wealthy, religious leaders, or the military. What complicates the meaning of democracy is its dynamic relationship to such notions as liberalism (which, again loosely explained, is the freedom of the individual to pursue his or her own vision of the good life), capitalism (market economies dependent on entre-

preneurial behavior), and such associated terms of governmental organization as *federal*, *republic*, and *representative*. The popular understanding of
democracy is often some hazy conglomeration of all these terms.

Fortunately we do not have to sort through the haze to put forward an
essential point: If the responsibility for governance rests with the people,
then the people must understand how to properly exercise that responsibility. Indeed, one the classic reasons for not vesting the people with the responsibility to govern is that they will make a mess of it. Plato, for example,
had a great distrust of democracy, fearing that if the masses had the authority to rule they would not act to advance enlightenment and good order.

This suspicion of democracy represented the standard view for many
centuries. In some ways, the full realization of the promise of democracy
had to await the rise of the nation-state and the development of a political
philosophy sufficient to guide political practice. Both of these were in place
at the time Europeans began to settle the American continent. Without in
any way diminishing the horrors that such settlement brought to Native
peoples in the Americas, the formation of the United States as a national
government became the first large-scale, practical experiment in democracy.

The nation's founders understood that realizing the promise of democracy depended absolutely on education. In order to rule, the people must
be prepared to do so. In Thomas Jefferson's famous words, "That nation
which expects to be both ignorant and free, in a state of civilization, expects
what never was and never will be." Education was clearly understood to be
the means for preparing the people for the responsibilities of democratic
citizenship. However, at the outset, "the people" included only White
males, usually property owning, and typically from western Europe or of
western European descent. One way to read the history of the United States
is as a continual struggle to enlarge that restricted franchise, so that eventually the opportunity to rule and the assurances of life, liberty, and the pursuit of happiness would be extended to *every* person.

Formal education has long served as the mechanism not only for
preparing the young to exercise the responsibilities of citizenship, but also
as the means for bringing more and more groups of people into the category of citizen rulers. The liberationist approach takes this responsibility seriously. Its commitment to justice and to the rule of law is one of its foundational pillars. The central argument, advanced eloquently by John Dewey
in his classic work *Democracy and Education*, is that democracy is to be trea-
sured as a form of government because it alone extends to each and every
person the opportunity to realize his or her full potential and render both
service and advancement to the entire human race. This potential cannot be
realized without education. Democracy and education are thus interdependent; indeed, they are synergistic. They keep redounding to the benefit of

one another. The more educated the people are, the more capable they become of governing in ways that amplify freedom, autonomy, and the pursuit of happiness. The more they perfect the mechanisms of democracy the more they are able to engage in education that enables the growth of human capacity and spirit.

It has too often been the case, however, that the promises of the dynamic synergy of education and democracy go unfulfilled. These failed promises motivate the emancipatory variant. The emancipationists, frustrated at the slow or retrograde pace of democratic progress, argue that it is not enough for the liberationists to merely prepare the young for thoughtful, discerning, morally good lives. They must also address directly the failures of social justice and moral principle that characterize life—not just in democratic societies, but around the world. Emancipationists seek to make the problems of social justice and moral goodness the foci of the curriculum. They grant the necessity of deep study in the disciplines and of the need for a manner proper to such study, but argue that education cannot stop with these. It must move on to praxis, to action grounded in high ideals and noble purpose. Given what we have already learned about the emancipationists, it comes as no surprise that their concerns for social justice are centrally located in matters of social class, power, and discriminatory practices rooted in race, culture, gender, disability, and sexual orientation.

Social Justice and Identity

In the previous chapter we discussed how the facilitator attends carefully to the formation of identity. To do so, the facilitator must be highly sensitive to those social and cultural factors that affect identity formation. Social class, race, gender, disability, and sexual orientation are among the more critical factors in identity formation that bear directly on the work of the school. The facilitator focuses on these factors because he wishes to guard against the intrusion of any impediments to the formation of a healthy, authentic identity. The emancipationist attends to these factors for a different reason.

The emancipationist addresses them as vital issues in need of improvement. In emancipationist teaching, these factors are made a direct part of the curriculum, to be studied, discussed, and eventually acted upon. Given the evident political orientation that so often accompanies emancipationist teaching, matters of social justice are taken very seriously.

Healthy identity formation is important to the emancipationist as well as to the facilitator, but for the latter, it is a "background" consideration unless the students themselves choose to bring it into the foreground. The emancipationist inclines more to the belief that the world would be vastly improved if such factors as race and gender were far less potent determinants of identity formation. To achieve this state of affairs, the emancipationist seeks a more just and equitable world, one that does not discriminate on the basis of race, gender, social class, disability, or sexual orientation.

This difference between the facilitator and the emancipationist also serves to illuminate a difference between the emancipationist and the liberationist. Because emancipationist teaching is grounded so strongly in praxis, in thought combined with action, the curriculum of the emancipationist is, as was already pointed out, more likely to be organized around problems rather than subjects. The emancipationist does not neglect subject matter, but calls upon it as a means of assisting in the resolution of problems. The liberationist, in contrast, depends on subject matter as a way to prepare the young to address issues and problems that arise in their own lives, as well as in such venues as the workplace and in the affairs of government.

The liberationist says, "Let us study and learn before we take on the burden of the world's problems." The emancipationist says, "Let us learn by studying and acting on the problems of the world." The liberationist is leery of engaging the young too quickly in the resolution of highly complex and contentious social and political problems, preferring instead to cultivate the skills necessary for successful negotiation of these problems. Political action, for the liberationist, requires experience and maturity, as well as wisdom and sensibility. We may not advantage either the young or the nation by making contentious social issues the focus of education. Of course, with this point of view, it may be that the liberationist is simply copping out. It may be that this approach is not suited to grappling with the profound disagreements that characterize contemporary life. Whether that is so must await the discussion in the following chapter, where we reexamine all three approaches and consider their pros and cons. Before turning to chapter 5, we encourage you to sharpen your understanding of the liberationist approach by working through the "Freedom and Indoctrination" dispute in chapter 7. In addition, check the other relevant cases indicated in table 2 of that chapter.

Chapter 5

Reflections on the Three Approaches

Now that all three approaches and their variations have been described, do you find that you prefer one over the others? Perhaps you find all three attractive. Or you might like some limited combination of approaches and their variations. And of course there is always the possibility that none of them appeals to you. Whatever your preferences at the moment, you should be aware that all three approaches and their variations have received extensive criticism over the years.

We purposely suppressed these negative perspectives in the previous chapters in order to allow each approach its "best shot" at capturing your attention and your desire to try teaching in that way. Yet it is very important to understand the arguments that detractors have lodged against the different approaches. Understanding what others believe to be the error in a particular approach not only adds to the depth of our understanding; it leads to a more balanced and careful use of the approach. In chapter 6 we will invite you to thoughtfully consider how you might make the best use of one or more of the approaches. First, however, we need to reassess the three approaches and their variations, paying particular attention to their potential downside consequences. Before we do so, we thought you might find it useful to have a summary of what has been covered so far.

A Synoptic View

The executive approach emphasizes well-managed classrooms with a focus on effective teaching leading to proficient learning. The facilitator approach places the student's development as an authentic, self-actualized person as its most important goal and assigns a high priority to the teacher's gaining a deep understanding of her students. The liberationist approach attends to the pursuit of high ideals of intellectual and moral accomplishment through deep study of the disciplines combined with appropriate manner on the part of the teacher.

Over the past several decades, two of the three primary approaches have developed variations. The facilitator approach has care pedagogy as its most contemporary variation, while the liberationist approach has emancipatory teaching as an alternative conception of freeing the person. In addition to these two major variations, we also noted how notions of constructivist teaching and multiple intelligences can deepen understanding of the facilitator approach. Finally, we discussed conceptions of diversity and multiculturalism as they appear in each of the three approaches. Much has been covered since you began your reading with the teaching vignettes of Jim Barnes, Nancy Kwong, and Roberto Umbras.

Using the MAKER framework, table 1 provides a quick summary of all three approaches, showing what elements are dominant in each approach and which are recessive.

The executive teacher, you will recall, places a high value on the body of knowledge that students are to acquire and attends to those methods of instruction that will most effectively lead to the acquisition of this body of knowledge. Thus M and K are dominant in this approach. Awareness of students, particularly their personal histories and interests, is addressed primarily as a means to determine how best to succeed with learning the subject matters of the school curriculum. Relationships have much the same status as awareness; they are forged primarily as a means to promote mastery of content. Ends, as you will recall, pertain to acquiring the knowledge and information contained within the curriculum of the school.[1]

The facilitative teacher values the healthy formation of the person over the mastery of school subjects. The facilitator assists students in becoming self-actualized, authentic persons, persons who have a sense of themselves and who will continue to grow on their own after their schooling has con-

Table 1. Summary of the Approaches Using the MAKER Framework

	Executive	Facilitator	Liberationist
Dominant	Method (M)	Awareness (A)	Knowledge (K)
	Knowledge (K)	Ends (E)	Ends (E)**
Recessive	Awareness (A)	Method (M)	Method (M)
	Ends (E)	Knowledge (K)	Awareness (A)
	Relationships (R)	Relationships (R)*	Relationships (R)

* Care pedagogy adds R to the dominant elements
** Emancipatory teaching alters some liberationist ends and changes the way K is pursued by students

cluded. To achieve these ends, facilitative teachers attend carefully to establishing a close, personal awareness of their students. Attention of this kind makes relationships important in the facilitator approach, but the concept of relationship is not nearly so well developed in the mainstream facilitator approach as it is in its variant, care pedagogy. Care pedagogy accords R the premier position in the MAKER scheme, as it grounds the work of the teacher in a profound regard for the student as person.

The liberationist teacher does not see a conflict between mastery of subject matter and the healthy development of the person. By addressing knowledge in its highly developed disciplinary forms and making careful use of manner, the liberationist strives for the formation of students who are highly capable in reasoning, judgment, and moral conduct. With these capacities, students are thereby prepared to both contemplate and pursue high, noble ideals of human possibility. Awareness and relationship in the repertoire of the liberationist are much as they are for the executive: They are addressed more as instrumental means to ends than as primary elements in one's approach to teaching. Method also is relegated to secondary status. For the liberationist, method is more likely to be determined by the form, structure, and methods of inquiry of the various disciplines of study than by psychological techniques that have been shown to promote mastery of a predefined curriculum.

Emancipatory teaching represents a variation on the liberationist approach by emphasizing action over contemplation. It typically addresses this orientation to action by making real social, political, and economic problems the focus of the curriculum and by introducing subjects of study as these bear on the resolution of the problems posed. In this variation, the noble ends of the liberationist are maintained, but their content is heavily influenced by ideals of social justice. Knowledge remains vital to the emancipationist, although addressed more as a basis for just action than for contemplation and the cultivation of wisdom. The emancipationist may attend carefully to awareness in the course of teaching, but such concentration is more often in the service of attaining the ends of social justice than it is in aiding the student to become what he or she seeks to be.

We hope that this summary has refreshed your memory of material already covered and helps to create a richer context for the analyses that follow. Turning now to these analyses, we discuss each approach in turn before moving to an overall consideration in chapter 6.

Critical Perspectives on the Executive Approach

As the assumptions and implications of the executive approach are studied in depth, certain disturbing things turn up. The teacher seems like the manager of a kind of production line, whereby students enter the factory as raw material and are somehow "assembled" as informed and knowledgeable persons. The teacher is not so much an actual part of the process as a manager of it. The teacher is not, it seems, "inside" the process of teaching and learning but "outside," where he regulates the content and the activities of the learner. Indeed, some critics have viewed the time-management aspects of the executive approach as akin to those of an oarmaster on an ancient slave ship—the one who stands, beating a large drum, to keep the rowers on-task.

These characterizations of the executive teacher—as factory manager, production-line supervisor, or slave-ship oarmaster—offend our sensibilities about education. Most of us do not like to think about children, school, and teaching along the lines of factories or slave ships. Yet the executive approach invites comparison to such things. It stresses attention to task, performance of duty, achievement of results, and accountability for failure to produce. The executive approach seems to disregard parts of education that many think are of utmost importance, such as the nature and interests of individual students, the special characteristics of different subject matters, and the varying demands that differences in geography, economics, and culture make on what takes place in school.

Another criticism of the executive approach is that it places too much emphasis on the acquisition of subject-matter knowledge and not enough on the good uses of this knowledge or on other purposes of schooling, such as attaining physical and emotional well-being, acquiring life skills (for example, managing credit, finding good work), and exercising democratic citizenship. Critics of the executive approach worry that highly knowledgeable people can often be found engaged in morally reprehensible undertakings (Nazi Germany is the oft-given example, but grievous scandals in the business and political sectors of our own country also illustrate the point). Knowledge alone, the critics argue, should never be the sole or most exalted end of education. The proper uses of knowledge, the exercise of moral virtue, and the care and nurture of fellow human beings and other creatures should be treated as ends deserving equal consideration.

What do you think? Do you see yourself as an executive teacher, despite these shortcomings? Or are you disappointed that what seemed a useful way to approach teaching turns out to have some unsavory features? If you favor the executive approach, what arguments might you offer in its defense? And if you are an advocate for this approach, where should you exercise caution? Let's take a look at some answers to these questions.

In the introductory chapter, you met Jim Barnes, the elementary school teacher who prided himself on his ability to teach specific subject matter. Imagine that you are Jim. You want your fifth-grade students to master computing the area of plane surfaces bounded by straight lines—that is, to learn the formula $(A = bh)$ and to be able to apply it correctly. You have a clear idea of the content (K) you want to get across, but how are you going to do it? Why not use the executive approach? It appears ideally suited to this outcome. In fact, it seems foolish not to approach this teaching task according to the executive approach. Bring the class together and get down to business right away, discuss the objective of this lesson, teach the lesson clearly and without exceeding the students' ability to comprehend you, assign seatwork so that students can practice what you are teaching them, monitor their seatwork closely, follow up with a presentation to clarify any lingering confusion, check for understanding, then test to determine whether they mastered the content. Could there be any better way?

Maybe. Think about some things that are missing from this little scenario. Do the students have any interest in computing the surface area? Are they able to perceive a value or use for this knowledge? Does Jim care very much about his lesson, or is he teaching it simply because it comes next in the adopted curriculum of the school? If you want answers to these questions, the executive approach is unlikely to offer them. Yet is it a powerful approach for getting across specific content. Moreover, as noted in chapter 2, it appears to be a good fit with the current educational-policy environment, an environment that places a premium on standards for learning; on frequent, standardized testing; and on comparing teachers and schools based upon results achieved on these tests. A good executive teacher is likely to be well regarded in the current school climate, because he has gained proficiency with an approach designed to produce the kind of results much sought after in these times.

The qualities that make the executive approach so appealing to some are the very characteristics that lead the facilitator and liberationist to raise objections to it. Too little attention to the learner as an autonomous, authentic learner, says the facilitator. Far too naive a sense of subject-matter knowledge, says the liberationist—and too little appreciation for the important role to be played by the manner of the teacher. These objections are sharpened in the following two sections.

Critical Perspectives on the Facilitator Approach

The facilitator is profoundly opposed to stuffing information into the heads of students, treating them as passive receptacles to be filled with whatever society believes it is important for them to know and be able to do. Instead, the facilitator is intent on students undergoing a journey of self-discovery and self-realization. Such journeys are possible only when the student is given a great deal of choice. That sounds like a wonderful approach to child rearing—until we ask a few pointed questions. How should educators handle the education of children too young to make informed choices? What should they do when a youngster decides against any further participation in schooling? What liberty should be given to the youngster who exhibits bigotry, meanness, or violence?

These questions suggest that there must be some limits to the personal liberty that the facilitator extends to her students. But where to draw the line? How do we know that the teacher is according her students enough freedom and autonomy to qualify as a facilitator, and how constrained may this freedom become before the teacher is no longer a facilitator? Consider, too, how easy it is to deceive oneself about being a facilitator. When students make the choices we believe they should make, we offer them more choices; in so doing, we might come to think of ourselves as facilitators. But when students choose directions to which we are opposed, we curtail their range of choices. In so doing, do we not reveal ourselves to be "fake" facilitators?

These questions and others like them plague the facilitator approach. Another example pertains to what is known as the "right-answer syndrome." Many teachers inclined to the executive approach are said to suffer from placing far too great an emphasis on right answers to questions posed by teacher, text, or test. Facilitators, in contrast, are less concerned with right answers, partly because facilitators place a higher value on the student's effort to engage material that is of interest to them and partly because the facilitator is aware that if the student feels too punished by wrong answers he or she may choose to opt out of the lesson. Yet how far may the facilitator go? Should errors of fact be allowed, be overlooked, or go uncorrected? Should poor writing or sloppy work be allowed to stand? Should inappropriate conduct go unnoticed or unpunished? Some advocates for facilitation argue that these absences and omissions are proper, that the facilitative approach is corrupted when the teacher strives for right answers or for work that meets externally imposed standards.

This tolerance for error, this allowance for so wide a margin of difference in style and quality of work, has been the target of extensive criticism leveled at the facilitator approach. There is a clearly a balance to be achieved here, but it is far from easy to obtain. Too much discretion yielded to the student risks the entire enterprise of educating that student; too little discretion risks failure in achieving the very goals that define the facilitator approach: self-actualization and authenticity.

These are not the only challenges confronting the facilitator. Another powerful rebuttal comes from those who argue that too exclusive an em-

phasis on the individual and on choice destroys one of the most fundamental purposes of schooling: to forge a common understanding and a
common bond among and between all the young people who reside in
this nation.

Forging National Identity

The facilitator approach shows extraordinary regard for allowing and encouraging each human being to come to terms with his or her own uniqueness. Indeed, that is the subtext, if you will, of self-discovery and self-actualization. As such, the facilitative teacher lacks the warrant to impose
(perhaps *indoctrinate* would not be too strong a term) ideas, ideologies, loyalties, and commitments upon students. Yet how does one forge cultural or
national identities without some degree of imposition? When children are
required to learn the stories of a nation in the process of forming itself,
when they are taught respect for the national flag and other symbols, when
they are told or read about national sacrifice in time of armed conflicts,
when they learn certain songs and recite particular pledges, these activities
shape their sentiments, identities, and loyalties.

In the United States it has long been accepted that the maintenance of
democracy and national identity requires a common education. The state,
in the form of both state and federal governments, presumes an entitlement to ensure the preservation of the nation and the ideals for which it
stands. As part of this entitlement, the state establishes schools whose
mission is, in part, to ensure that those about to become citizens understand the history of the nation, grasp its fundamental principles and
ideals, and accept the necessity of defending these principles and ideals
when they are under threat. On this basis the state presumes that it is justified in imposing certain understandings and perspectives on the young
(with the further understanding—in democracies such as the United
States—that upon becoming citizens, persons may work for change, even
revolution, should leaders and policies fail to live up to foundational
principles and ideals).

The facilitator approach is sharply challenged by imposition and even
the slightest hint of indoctrination. Thus the forging of a national identity
in the setting of the school is highly problematic for the facilitative
teacher. Perhaps the challenge can be surmounted through the argument
that forging national identity is a transcendent purpose of school, and
therefore should be allowed as an exception to facilitative principles. On
this argument, the facilitative teacher says something like, "OK, I will
allow imposition to occur for purposes of forging national identity, but
only for that purpose. In all other matters of knowledge and ends, I shall

strive to the extent possible to allow student needs and interests to prevail." Readers will, we are sure, recognize how slippery a slope is a response of this kind. Once again, the line becomes exceedingly hard for the facilitator to draw.

It is of no small interest to inquire how the other approaches respond to this issue of forging national identity through the imposition of a common set of stories, songs, symbols, and pledges. Pause a moment to think it through. Where does the executive stand? The liberationist? The emancipationist? We offer a few brief answers, encouraging you to develop them further than we do here.

Imposition is not problematic for the executive approach, provided that it is neither extreme nor excessive. However, we want to take care to point out that we do not mean that the executive is in favor of indoctrination (the word has such negative connotations in these times, but if you ponder it carefully, you will find that all approaches depend upon it to some extent as an educational device, to be used modestly and with care). While no less considerate of truth, evidence, and integrity than are teachers who represent the other approaches, the executive understands that, in large part, the curriculum, the standards for its attainment, and many of the means for its implementation are determined elsewhere and given over to the teacher for pursuit in the classroom. Thus the executive is not likely to be too troubled by the imposition of certain pledges, stories, and symbols that most would agree are a part of our national heritage.

The liberationist is more resistant to imposition but is likely to look with favor on the need to forge a common national identity. In the hands of the liberationist, this process will be carried out with argument and analysis. The liberationist will contend that if the principles and ideals withstand intellectual scrutiny and emerge with strong justification for adoption, then they should be accepted by students. The liberationist teacher may also draw a distinction between blind patriotism and reasoned acceptance of foundational freedoms and principles. Yet he might also make a move similar to that of the facilitator, arguing that issues of national identity are so compelling that they justify a measure of imposition. Perhaps the liberationist will further justify this stance with the claim that there is not enough time or opportunity to subject everything to deep analysis, and thus a measure of imposition is permissible, especially on matters of high common purpose that are backed by an extensive national consensus. Such compromises are often the reality in the context of complex and multiple demands made upon schooling, although it is important to be aware that one has stepped outside the rules and principles of one's approach to teaching when making such adjustments to how content is taught.

Can you imagine the reaction of the emancipationist to any such compromise by the liberationist, facilitator, or executive? If you answered that it would be outrage, you would be correct. The emancipationist turns the curriculum into problems to be studied, worked through, and acted upon in a concerted effort to avoid imposition. For the emancipationist, every topic of instruction should be open to scrutiny, particularly those pertaining to politics, culture, and economy. Indeed, the emancipationist frets that the imposition of identity and loyalty is often undertaken to hide injustices in treatment and other abuses of power and privilege. The risk that is always carried by accepting the need for the imposition of certain valued principles and positions is that the interests of the privileged and the powerful will be served while those of the less fortunate and able will be subverted.

These reflections on liberationist and emancipationist responses to the forging of national identity provide a segue into the last section of this chapter. We turn now to critical reactions to the third approach to teaching.

Critical Perspectives on the Liberationist Approach

The liberationist's intense focus on the disciplines of knowledge has troubled many who have looked closely at this approach. They ask whether it is truly possible or even desirable for all students to study the core subjects in the way that is advocated by the liberationist, especially given the broad range of individual differences in most classrooms. They express doubt that all students require or are even capable of this probing initiation into human forms of knowledge and understanding. While such criticism opens the possibility of charges of elitism and snobbery in the liberationist approach, it also exposes another challenge. That challenge involves a certain narrowness in view of what is meant by an educated person.

Jane Roland Martin, a philosopher of education who has done a great deal to illuminate the impact of feminist philosophy on educational practice, worries that the liberationist view encapsulates a sense of education that is far too spare and constrained. She attacks the standard bearers for liberationist teaching (particularly Hirst and Peters, whose views we mentioned in the previous chapter), contending that they are too ivory tower, too cognitive and cerebral in form and content. She writes:

> The great irony of Hirst's theory of liberal education is that it is neither tolerant nor generous; it conceives of liberal education as the development of mind, restricts the development of mind to the acquisition of knowledge

and understanding, and restricts knowledge to true propositions. . . . The received theory's liberally educated person will be taught to see the world through the lenses of the seven forms of knowledge, if seven there be, but not to act in the world. Nor will that person be encouraged to acquire feelings and emotions. The theory's liberally educated person will be provided with knowledge about others, but will not be taught to care about their welfare, let alone to act kindly toward them. That person will be given some understanding of society, but will not be taught to feel its injustices or even to be concerned over its fate.[2]

You may have detected some flavor of care pedagogy and perhaps even the emancipatory variation on the liberationist approach in this quotation. Both are indeed there, as feminist philosophy often picks up elements of care theory and radical critique (the latter has roots in Marxist and postmodernist theory). In this case, Martin chastises the proponents of liberationist teaching for failing to embrace the notion of a person as someone with a particular kind of character and emotional set, and as someone who is not just an individual with a facile mind but also a contributing member of a sustaining community. It is not so much a matter of objecting to the ends set forth by the liberationist as it is that these ends are too narrow, too unidimensional in their portrayal of human capacity and human goodness.

Narrowness in conception of human capacity and potential is among the more serious objections to the liberationist approach. Another serious objection was touched on just above, the potential for elitism. One of the more fascinating features of liberationist teaching is that it feeds off itself, in the sense that the more education a person has, the more robustly and effectively a teacher can engage that student in the pursuit of the ends of liberation. Thus persons of advantage—typically those with social-class standing, privilege, or power—who arrive at the schoolhouse door ready to read and calculate, and who have a head start on logical thought and verbal expression, are more likely than others to be the beneficiaries of the liberationist approach. It is with such well-prepared beginners that the teacher can readily launch probing examinations of the disciplines and embark on journeys of intellectual and moral discovery.

The ease with which liberationist teaching can be undertaken with students who are advantaged by prior nurturing of educationally relevant skills may, and unfortunately often does, have the result of providing these students with liberationist teaching while denying such teaching to others (for some general examples, consider the practice in many secondary schools of segregating students into various academic tracks, or the eligibility granted to some students for enrollment in advanced placement [AP] courses while others are counseled into courses of a general or vocational nature). Thus it often turns out that liberationist teaching is accorded to the children of advantage, thereby leading to the charge of elitism.

The charge of elitism is an ironic one for the liberationist, as a grounding principle of the liberationist approach is that it can and should be made accessible to all children. Jerome Bruner's famous words in his now classic book *The Process of Education*, that "any subject can be taught effectively in some intellectually honest form to any child at any stage of development,"[3] reiterate a view that has long been a standard for liberationists. They believe that all children have the capacity to learn and so should have equality of access to "the funded capital of civilization" (John Dewey's words). Still, there is something about this approach that, once entangled with the social and political realities of schooling, results in a partitioning of its provision and its benefits. Have we explained the position well enough for you to speculate why that might be so? We will not say more here, but hope you will continue to ponder the question.

Given what you know about the emancipationist variation, it likely comes as no surprise that they are among the leaders in the charge of elitism, despite their close connection with the high ideals of the liberationist. The emancipationist has been especially sensitive to the dynamic between the liberationist approach and the social-class systems of developed, industrialized nations. Emancipationists seek to alter this dynamic by attending carefully to ends embedded in social justice, orienting the curriculum of the school to problems arising from class, race, gender, income disparity, disability, and so forth. Thus they evidence a special concern for providing children lacking in advantage with the skills and insight needed to gain access to bodies of knowledge and skills from which they are typically restricted.

As is so often the case with strongly normative approaches, the very core of the emancipationist variation becomes the target of most of the criticism directed at it. It is, many argue, too ideological, too politicized, for adoption in the context of educating children in a society that values ideological neutrality in the schooling of its children and youth. For others, the objection lies not so much in that it is political as in what kind of politics it is—left wing, radical, even socialist—in the minds of many detractors.

Its ideological character is not the only objection lodged against the emancipationist. Another is that it is inadequately conceived as a pedagogy. It is not at all clear what one does, as activities of teaching, when one embraces emancipatory teaching. The ends appear clear enough, but how these are converted to teaching practices is still vague and incomplete (although there has been some progress on this score, as the works cited in note 12 for chapter 4 demonstrate). Almost as troubling as the lack of an explicit pedagogy is the challenge of adequately covering the required curriculum when using a problem-oriented focus for the presentation of academic content. The general emancipationist strategy in the classroom is to "problematize" (a term employed by emancipationists with some frequency) curriculum topics, turning them into issues for the students to confront. While doing so offers the emancipationist an explicit means to pursue desired ends, the strategy typically requires an extensive amount of time and participation per issue or topic. That leaves uncovered a lot of material, much of which might be needed for students to succeed at subsequent studies or in later grades (or to earn good scores on standardized tests).

The emancipationist's attention to matters of social justice, although often as much a challenge as an advantage for this variation, does call our attention back to this very important aspect of contemporary education. Before bringing these reflections on the three approaches to a close, we would like to return to matters multicultural, doing what we can to bring together notions of democracy, diversity, and identity—notions that have so far been discussed piecemeal.

Democracy, Identity, and Diversity

One of the more significant challenges faced by education in these times is how to balance regard for difference (often known as *pluralism* or *diversity*) with a sense of what is common to a nation, its people, and its government. Many political theorists believe that in a political system such as that in place in the United States, holding certain things in common across all the people is essential to sustaining a healthy, fully functioning democracy (a perspective we explored just a few pages back). John Dewey put it in just this way in his famous work *Democracy and Education*. He envisioned progress toward becoming a more democratic society being dependent upon the increasing degree to which various groups shared common interests and basic values, and on the increasing freedom with which groups interacted with one another based upon these common interests and values. For some, however, valuing pluralism and diversity threatens this commonness, replacing it with such a range of differences that democratic governance becomes impossible to maintain. Viewed in this way, the challenge seems to be either commonness or pluralism, democracy or diversity.

There is, of course, an alternative resolution. It involves finding a balance between the need for commonality in order to sustain the benefits of liberty and self-governance, and the need for difference in order to permit various cultures, languages, and value orientations to survive, even flourish. How, for example, do we support the Latino interest in the Spanish language and a culture other than the dominant American one, while ensuring sufficient commonality to sustain democratic governance? Questions much like this one can be raised for all groups asserting a difference between themselves and a common or dominant culture. Such questions may also go beyond race, ethnicity, and language, to issues of gender, physical and mental condition, religious belief, sexual orientation, and age.

This is clearly one of the central issues of our time, and as for many other such issues, schools are a prime site for adjudicating and resolving the problems inherent in it. Often however, while the larger society is in the process of debating how such matters should be handled in law, in policy, and in everyday life, schoolteachers are expected to have some settled, preferably noncontroversial ways of dealing with these same issues. Hence the need for helpful ways to think through the contested claims in order to find workable resolutions. Do the three approaches described in this book offer such help? Yes, most of them do. To make clear how they do requires "backing up" a bit, gaining a broader perspective on the issues at hand.

For 200 years American democracy has survived, perhaps thrived, on a commonality rooted in ideas and values characteristic of western European cultures. This common heritage is generally regarded as White, privileged, Christian, and male. Shifting attention to difference and diversity is believed to pose a threat to the cohesive dominance of the Eurocentric, primarily Christian, privileged male view of how the political economy of the United States should be managed. The issues that are seen as so troublesome for us in these times may be thought of as arising from the tension between the dominant ideology that has traditionally formed the American commons and the newer demands for recognition of perspectives different from the dominant one. The confounding problem for many is whether commons and difference can coexist in good democratic order, and whether they may even be mutually sustaining of one another.

It could be said that what the United States, and many other developed nations, are in the process of discovering is how to scrap a single-perspective commons for a multiple-perspective one. That is, how can a commons be formed and sustained, and how does it in turn sustain democratic order, if it consists of multiple, frequently conflicting, often irreconcilable points of view on such critical issues as who we are, what we stand for, and where we are trying to go as a nation? The answer to this question is, for many, not yet at hand, while others believe either that it is impossible to find or that is has been staring us in the face for some time.

The two strongly normative approaches we have discussed here, the facilitator and the liberationist, and each of their variations, leave little doubt about the course to be taken. Recognition of and respect for difference is a hallmark of democracy, and democracies that give serious attention to working out the challenges that difference and diversity present will be far stronger for doing so. One can find justification of this position within the concepts and principles that guide the facilitator approach and its care variant as well as the liberationist approach and its emancipatory variant. Care pedagogy and emancipatory teaching address the issues more directly, but facilitative and liberationist teaching are filled with principled implications that leave no doubt about where they stand on this matter.

The executive approach, as an approach, is neutral on the matter. Given that it is the least normative of the three approaches, that is to be expected. The executive teacher may take a strong stand for or against diversity and difference, and not be in violation of the approach itself. There is an exception to this claim, however. Can you think what it might be? (Take a moment to form an answer before reading on.)

If attending to diversity and difference were shown to have positive effects on students mastering the content taught, then respect for difference and diversity would occupy a powerful position within the executive approach. Whether or not it does have such an effect is one of the contested educational-research issues of the past several decades. Some argue that research shows that such programs as bilingual education, ethnocentric schooling, and multicultural education do have positive effects on student achievement. Others disagree. The dispute, regardless of outcome, reveals just how powerful an influence scientific research has on the executive approach and how strongly the facilitator and liberationist approaches are influenced by their more normative underpinnings.

Does this discussion of democracy and diversity persuade you more of one of the approaches or its variations than of the others? Do you feel prepared to make a decision on what kind of teacher you wish to be? We hope so. But before you bring your thoughts to a conclusion, we would like you to consider becoming all three.

Chapter 6

Developing Your Approach to Teaching

In this brief chapter we explore the connections between the three approaches, then consider how you might employ them as either ways to examine someone else's teaching or as approaches to your own teaching. The chapter concludes with our hope for your success as a teacher. We begin with the question of whether the three approaches are incompatible with one another. In other words, can you adopt more than one approach without being inconsistent or contradicting yourself?

Three Ideas, Three Approaches

In a work titled *The Educated Mind: How Cognitive Tools Shape Our Understanding*,[1] Kieran Egan contends that educational theory is rooted in just three ideas: "that we must shape the young to the current norms and conventions of adult society, that we must teach them the knowledge that will ensure their thinking conforms with what is real and true about the world, and that we must encourage the development of each student's individual potential."[2] Did you note the parallels between Egan's three "significant educational ideas" and the three approaches?

His sequencing is just a bit different from ours, but the three approaches are well represented. The first idea is that the purpose of education is to "shape the young to the current norms and conventions of adult society." We trust that evoked a remembrance of the executive approach, for that is an important consequence of this approach. The second idea is to instruct students so that "their thinking conforms with what is real and true about the world." This second idea, which Egan attributes to Plato, is akin to the liberationist approach. The third idea, the development of each student's potential, is attributed to Rousseau, whose classic work *Émile* describes the rearing of a child in the most pristine, natural circumstances possible. This third idea is, of course, very much the facilitator approach to teaching.

Now the interesting part. After taking note of these three ideas, Egan writes: "The good news, I suppose, is that there are indeed only three ideas to grasp. The bad news is that the three ideas are mutually incompatible" (p. 3). Are they indeed incompatible? We seem to have suggested all along that they are, but perhaps that is an erroneous view. In an effort to answer the question, we look first at Egan's defense for his view.

The executive approach is incompatible with the liberationist approach because the former fosters compliance and conformity, while the latter fosters skepticism and autonomy. Athens compelled Socrates, Plato's teacher, to drink hemlock because he was corrupting the morals of the youth, encouraging them to question, to think for themselves. In other words, Athens sought conformity to its societal norms and values, while Socrates and Plato preferred to question these values in pursuit of what they believed to be the higher goods of knowledge, truth, and beauty.

The liberationist approach is, in turn, incompatible with the facilitator approach because the former honors a fixed and established body of knowledge (what we have referred to as the disciplines), while the latter selects the knowledge to be acquired based on the needs and interests of the learner. Egan characterizes this tension between the followers of Plato and those of Rousseau as follows:

> The former argue for a more structured curriculum, logically sequenced, and including the canonical knowledge of Western "high" culture; the latter argue for activities that encourage students to explore the world around them and, in as far as they are willing to prespecify curriculum content, they propose knowledge relevant to students' present and likely future experience. (p. 23)

After describing the tensions between the three ideas, Egan makes a remark that might well describe what you were thinking as you completed the previous chapters:

> Clearly few teachers adhere to one position to the exclusion of others; most teachers try to balance all of them in practice. So, for example, even Rousseau-inclined teachers tend to acknowledge the importance of the canonical content of the Plato-influenced curriculum; their compromise between incompatibles means that they feel it is important to "expose" students to the "high culture" curriculum content but they feel no imperative to persist with it for students who do not take to it. That is, each idea is allowed enough scope to undercut the other. (p. 23)

Egan believes that they are incompatible, that each "undercuts the other." We disagree. The defense of our position follows.

Becoming All Three

If we have done a good job presenting these three approaches, you found some features of each that you like and some that you do not. Perhaps you have formed a clear preference for one, or maybe narrowed your preferences to two and are trying to decide between them. If you are thinking of the approaches in this way, you are treating them as styles of teaching, in contrast to analytical lenses. You might remember this distinction from chapter 1, but just in case you do not, the following paragraph should refresh your memory.

From the styles of teaching perspective, the approaches are teaching persona. They are professional roles that you can adopt as a classroom teacher. As such, it may be that one appeals to you more than the others, and you want your teaching practices to be in accord with this approach. From the analytical-lens perspective, however, the approaches are schemata or frames for the study and appraisal of teaching. As seen from this second perspective, the approaches are not persona from which you might choose, but analytical devices for helping you to understand and make judgments about the various activities of teaching.

It is interesting that the approaches are typically treated as lenses when we are observing someone else's teaching, but as styles of teaching when we are considering our own teaching. That is, we use the approaches as lenses to understand and evaluate another's teaching, but as choices for a teaching persona when considering our own teaching. Given this duality of frames, one might conclude that it is important to understand all three approaches if one is analyzing someone else's teaching, but that it is both reasonable and acceptable to select one approach when deciding on the kind of teacher one wishes to be.

We shall argue to the contrary, at least with respect to choosing one approach to guide your own teaching. We believe that it is important for you to be comfortable with all three approaches, even though, like the elements in the MAKER framework, one approach might be dominant at a given time while the others are recessive. Although you may have a preferred approach, situations will arise that call for you to make the preferred approach recessive, while bringing a different approach to the fore. Practicing and gaining expertise in all three approaches prepares you to function well in different school settings, with different learners, who are in various stages of development at any given moment and posses a huge diversity of temperaments, needs, and interests.

How can we maintain this position in the face of Egan's counterargument? By making a distinction between incompatibilities in theory and incompatibilities in practice. What appears to be mutually exclusive or inconsistent in theory is not always that way in practice. Egan correctly assesses the incompatibility of these approaches in their theoretical mode, but does not allow for their compatibility in practice—where the approaches are not used simultaneously, but sequentially and contextually. That is, the teacher is in the persona of an executive with her class on this particular Tuesday because that is what seems the best approach for the tasks at hand. However, in individual consultations with Juan or Serene during the lesson she is using her facilitator persona, while with Tyler she decides to adopt a liberationist stance. On another day, perhaps with a different class, she is an emancipationist, while in individual or small-group interactions elements of other approaches are dominant.

It is reasonable and, we think, proper, for teachers to adopt one approach as a generally preferred approach. It is also reasonable and proper that the teacher will embellish this approach with stylistic features that are distinctive of his personality. However, the teachers we have observed whom we regard as especially accomplished are those who can, with relative ease and proficiency, take on other teaching personas that are the right match to the time and situation in which they find themselves. We think of these teachers as "wow teachers" because after we walk away from observing in their classrooms, we find ourselves saying, "Wow, what a teacher!" They are masters of their art, in the way great orchestra conductors, great surgeons, and great leaders are masters of their art.

Good-bye

We began this book, way back in "A Note to the Reader," with congratulations to those readers who are preparing to be teachers. You have chosen a career filled with extraordinary opportunities for wonder and reward. The reward comes in two parts: what you make possible for your students and what you make possible for yourself. One of the grand benefits of teaching is that you are reflected in every student and every class you have. If you open your eyes to that reflection, attending to it as if it were a gift, you gain something very precious. That is, the chance to refashion yourself again and again, always becoming more of what you want to be as both teacher and person.

The nature of schooling, as an institution and organization, does not make it easy for you or your students to see and refashion themselves. If you are not "awake" to the possibilities you have—to the different approaches to teaching from which you can choose—the great benefits of teaching can be replaced by the dulling routines and bureaucratic frustrations so common to large institutions in modern society. It is our hope that this little book has provided some of what you will need to both see the possible worlds of the exceptional teacher and become a "wow teacher" yourself.

To those experienced classroom teachers who may be among our readers, we thank you for the opportunity to illuminate different ways of understanding and undertaking the activities of teaching. Our intent has been to offer you new avenues for reflection as well as new topics for conversation with fellow teachers. To the extent we have succeeded in doing so, our aspirations will be fulfilled. Our thanks for the great service you render the nation and its children.

Chapter 7

Cases and Disputes

To this point we have examined three approaches to teaching and have asked you to think about them along the way. Each has much to commend it, and yet each has potential negative features. To help you reflect on and develop your own examined approach to teaching, this last chapter contains a series of realistic vignettes—in the form of cases, dialogues, and disputes—that raise a number of issues, including ethical ones not dealt with extensively or directly in the text. As you read them and discuss them with others, you will have an opportunity to articulate and examine some of your most heartfelt beliefs about teaching. They will also give you the opportunity to bring theory and practice closer together by showing you that how one thinks about and how one approaches one's teaching make a real difference in how one acts and reacts as a teacher in real-life situations.

To give you an overview of the topics we have treated and the major points at issue in them, we have provide a summary (see table 2) from which you can select cases and disputes of interest to you.

Some of you may have already sampled these cases and disputes when following the suggestions we made throughout the text. To indicate our recommendations of issues related to specific chapters, we have placed a chapter number in parentheses following the title of each case or dispute. Of course, you should feel free to use them in any order suitable to your interests and purposes or to write your own cases and disputes that bring issues from your own experiences into your class discussions. Many of the cases and disputes in this chapter reach beyond the neat conceptual lines drawn around the three approaches described earlier in the text, demonstrating that the real world of education is not as neatly packaged as textbooks and scholars sometimes make it out to be. This is not to say that thinking initially about teaching in terms of the heuristic scheme of the three approaches dealt with in this book is useless. Rather, it is to warn that when theory and reality meet, you need to accommodate your categories and schemata to the world in which you live and work, making reasonable adjustments that will allow you to pursue your most basic beliefs and values. We also hope that you will see that whatever name you give to your own approach to teaching is not as important as what you really believe about the purposes of teaching and what it means to be an educated per-

Table 2. Summary of Cases and Disputes

Page	Title*	Issue
78	Grading Policies (1)	Do different approaches call for different kinds of student evaluation?
79	School and Approach Mismatch (1)	Should a teacher change his or her approach to be more in line with school policies?
80	Teacher-Engineer or Artist? (2)	Is teaching an art or a science?
82	Individualized Learning (2)	Does research provide infallible material and techniques?
83	How Much Control Is Too Much? (2)	What are the advantages and disadvantages of the executive approach?
83	Workbook Dilemma (2)	Should the teacher or the administrator be the executive?
84	A New Science Kit (2)	Do curriculum materials reflect a techno-logical mindset and limit teacher creativity?
86	Individual and Social Needs (3)	Can the school serve both individual and social needs without conflict?
86	Curing Shyness (3)	Who determines the direction of personal growth, teacher or student?
87	What Standard Shall We Use? (3)	Should a teacher grade on personal growth and individual progress?
89	Teaching "Relevant" Literature (3)	What happens if students object to a teacher's approach?
90	Teachers and Mother? (3)	What happens if a teacher's personality and approach do not fit?
90	Freedom and Indoctrination (4)	Can the mind ever really become free through education?
91	Too Young to Be Critical? (4)	Is developing a critical mind age related?
92	Education for Life (4)	Is a liberal education for everyone?
93	Freedom of Speech? (4)	How open minded must a teacher using the liberationist approach be?
95	Mass or Class Culture? (4)	Is the liberationist approach elitist?
96	Learning Chemistry by Discussion (5)	Is the liberationist manner efficient?
98	Different Learning Styles (5)	What factors decide choice of approach?
98	Compatibility of Approaches (5)	Must a teacher choose an approach?
99	E Pluribus Unum (5)	How can a teacher respect diversity and yet teach for national identity?
100	Go Fly a Kite (1 and 6)	What happen when teachers use different approaches to the same school project?

* A number in parentheses after a title indicates that the case or dispute is recommended for use with that specific chapter.

son. Therefore, we hope you will use these cases and disputes as a bridge to the real world so that you may become a thinking and responsible teacher no matter what your approach.

Grading Policies

David Levine is the chairperson of Henry Hudson High School's social studies department. Because of the size of the student population, several sections of certain courses are offered each year, and each is taught by a different instructor. In the case of Modern American History, three teachers offer courses. Students are assigned to these courses according to a simple alphabetical rotation. But this simple system has created a complex problem for Mr. Levine, for each teacher uses a different approach, and parents and students are complaining that this is unfair.

The first section is taught by Albert Foley. Mr. Foley is a young, somewhat idealistic teacher who believes that stimulating learning experiences form the core of an education. In his class, he relies upon the study of current events from newspapers and television, and he encourages his students to initiate independent-study projects. Mr. Foley is not as concerned about command of exact facts as he is about the personal significance that modern American history may come to hold for his students. In that direction, he believes, lies the promise of good citizenship and authentic personhood. Students are graded on the basis of essays they write about topics they select and journals of personal response to classroom discussion and current events. He grades because he has to, but he does not believe that grading is what education is really about. Among the students, he is known as "Easy A. Foley." In a typical year, 40 percent of his students will receive *A*'s and another 30 percent will receive *B*'s. The rest are given *C*'s, with an occasional *D* for serious cases. Mr. Foley says that any student will pass his class who is able to find his or her way to the classroom. In his opinion, it is hard enough being a teenager, and he is not going to make it any tougher. He believes that his students really learn and grow in their sense of self-worth because of his teaching and grading policies.

"Historical knowledge broadens and deepens the mind" might be the motto of Mr. William Sampson, the teacher of the second section, for he believes that history is all important in getting students to understand the world they have inherited. Mr. Sampson uses textbooks containing primary sources, and he delivers detailed lectures. He demands that his students know the facts about American government and recent historical events, and he has little patience with uninformed opinions. He wants his students to use evidence from historical events and documents to back up their claims. In his view, good citizenship must rest on a solid foundation of knowledge and the ability to think critically. He tells his students that they will be graded on their ability to present sound arguments for their interpretations of historical events. His exams are not on the specific facts of history. Rather, he gives rigorous and demanding essay exams that force his students to think about history. In a recent class of forty students, Mr. Sampson's grades were distributed in the following manner: three *A*'s, five *B*'s, eighteen *C*'s, nine *D*'s, and five *F*'s. Mr. Sampson contends that his tests are fair measures of his students' ability to think. The students call him "Slasher Sampson."

Nancy Wright, the teacher of the third section, has taught history for twelve years, and each year she tries out new ideas and techniques she has read about in *Social Studies,* a national journal for teachers. This year she has developed a behavioral-objectives unit on the New Deal and has designed an evaluation instrument for it that gives her a very accurate assessment of a student's knowledge of FDR's policies. She has found that specifying her own objectives not only helps her but also helps her students see clearly what they need to study and learn in her classes. Each year she feels that her teaching is still improving. One thing she does not change, however, is her policy of grading according to a curve. In her most recent group of forty students there were five *A*'s, ten *B*'s, fifteen *C*'s, seven *D*'s, and three *F*'s, a distribution of grades that she came to favor long ago after taking a course on statistics and evaluation. Ms. Wright uses both essays and objective tests designed by curriculum experts in order to provide an unbiased basis for her judgments. She believes that her proportional approach to grading accurately reflects the performance of each student as it compares with that of others in the class. Ms. Wright's students have no nickname for her.

Consider these different approaches to teaching and grading. Do you favor one over another? Why? Does each approach necessitate the kind of evaluation procedure used by each teacher, or could each use one another's grading policy without altering their approach very much? Does an approach also dictate the content in a course? Is this situation as it now exists fair to the students? What would you do if you were Mr. Levine?

School and Approach Mismatch

Janet had taught history for several years at a junior college. Tired of lecturing and longing for a change, she decided to try working at a different level in the education system. The public schools were not hiring, so she accepted a job with a small, conservative, church-affiliated secondary school at a considerable reduction in salary, even though she was neither conservative nor religious. She agreed to teach four sections of freshman history and one of remedial junior English, with a total of 43 students.

Janet found teaching high school challenging and exciting. She liked being with the students and even relished lunchroom duty, because it afforded her the opportunity to observe student interaction and to interact herself. Accustomed to dealing with adults and high school graduates, she treated her students with respect and genuine care. In a short time she developed an easy relationship with her classes and became known as an adult who could be approached. Janet made a habit of coming to work early every day in order to be available for those students who wanted to shoot the breeze or needed to talk seriously. There was usually someone waiting for her, occasionally a student other than one of her own or even a fellow teacher.

As much as she loved and was rewarded by her work, she found dealing with the school's administration to be very difficult. Janet's personal philosophy of education emphasized discovery, opening the world for the student. She attempted to create a proper relaxed atmosphere for this. The school's position stressed adherence to rules, deference to authority, and strict norms of acceptable behavior. There was a rigid curriculum that was to be dispensed by the teacher and learned by the students. Teachers were responsible for seeing to it that all students learned this material. A proper distance between teacher and students was always to be maintained.

Janet soon found herself in conflict with the administration over these policies. Each classroom had a two-way speaker, and it was known that the principal and the attendance secretary occasionally listened in on class sessions. During the third week of school, Janet had been called on the carpet for allowing excessive noise in her classroom. When she apologized to her neighbors, she discovered that the complaint had not come from them but from the attendance secretary, who had been eavesdropping on the public-address system. Her colleagues also told her that the principal was dissatisfied because she was not covering the prescribed curriculum. Janet was furious about the way her teaching had been "observed."

Janet obviously faced a year at school in which she would often be acting in ways directly opposed to administrative goals and philosophy. But she needed her job.

In light of that economic reality, ought Janet to change her approach to teaching to be more in line with the administration's? Might it be possible to find a compromise approach? Should a teacher compromise his approach when it does not match the school's philosophy? What about professional autonomy and integrity? Do you think the "observation system" in this school is proper? What would you do if you were Janet?

Teacher–Engineer or Artist?

A: The practical importance of science is clear. It provides us with knowledge we can use in curing diseases, in exploring space, and in helping students learn. Education, no less than medicine or space exploration, must rest on a solid foundation of knowledge about how to do it.

B: I don't deny that knowledge about teaching like time on-task or how to design valid multiple-choice questions can be useful to a teacher. But when you come right down to it, teaching is an art. You can know your subject matter and materials, have a good grasp of learning theory and methods, and know the latest research findings, but when you're there in the classroom, your performance has to be more like an artist's than like a mechanical engineer's. Each teacher is a unique person, and it is by being yourself that you really become a good teacher.

A: A good teacher is an effective teacher, a teacher whose students learn! That can only happen if you think about your goals, carefully plan your lessons, select the appropriate techniques you will use, and exercise good judgment as you're teaching. If that is like being an *engineer*, so be it. It's not your artistic uniqueness that's important, it's your knowledge, experience, and executive ability that counts.

B: But what about those unanticipated teachable moments, those unplanned things the teacher as artist does that really get students excited about learning? What makes teaching come alive is the artistic talent of the really good teacher, not what she knows about the "science of teaching."

C: You both make good points. I'm not sure you really can separate the artistic from the scientific in any serious human endeavor. The good surgeon is as much artist as scientist and so is the good teacher.

A: If, by calling a surgeon an artist, you mean that he effectively executes his skills, I would agree. But that just makes my point. Both the surgeon and the teacher depend on the knowledge gained through research that proves one technique or method better than another, more effective in curing patients or in getting students to learn. It is the scientific knowledge that makes it possible to get the best results.

B: But don't you see what you're both assuming, that a better teacher is simply one who *produces* more learning regardless of subject matter and regardless of effects on students? That's a one-sided, mechanical view of teaching. An artistic view seeks to make the educational experience of students more self-fulfilling, more personally relevant, and more satisfying, and only a sensitive artist can do that.

A: Would you rather be evaluated as a teacher on an agreed-upon set of competencies you are expected to demonstrate by means of an instrument developed and validated for the purpose—or by some "art critic" supervisor who may or may not like your brand of art?

How would you prefer to be evaluated as a teacher? As an artist? As an engineer? Do you think that someone who takes the executive approach to teaching is less inclined to see things other than learning goals as important in teaching? What might such other things be?

Individualized Learning

Bob was a first-year teacher in a fifth-grade open classroom. Bob, like all the other teachers of his teaching team, had responsibility for one homogeneously grouped math class. The math program of the school was designed according to the latest research in the following manner: Each student progressed through a series of worksheets; when one worksheet was finished correctly, the student went to the next. In this way, skill in addition, subtraction, multiplication, and other areas was to be learned at an individual's own pace. The idea was that the teacher could give individual attention to those children who needed it. Research had shown that at this grade level, individualization was most effective.

Bob thought this system made sense. The students seemed to like the class, too. They were rewarded by the evidence of their progress and by the praise Bob gave when papers were completed.

Before long, though, Bob began to be uneasy about the direction his math class was taking. He felt that he was not really "teaching" his students. They were just doing worksheets on their own. He had thought he would be able to work one-on-one with the children. Instead, he found he spent almost no time with anyone. There was constantly a line of five or six children either waiting to ask questions or waiting to have papers checked. Bob felt that he could not afford to give as much time to each child as he would have liked, since it would be unfair to keep all the others waiting. The children who finished papers were congratulated and sent on to the next worksheet. The students who had questions were told to try to work out an answer by themselves. They often would, but this usually took the form of three or four unsuccessful guesses before the correct answer was stumbled upon. Furthermore, Bob was so busy at his desk that he had difficulty being sure students were working and behaving as they should. Some students seemed to be progressing much too slowly. Bob was concerned that this was because he had not watched these pupils closely enough. In short, Bob came to see himself less as a teacher and more as a "paper pusher."

Bob's worst fears seemed to be realized one day when he held an addition game. Bob chose problems that all the students should have known, since they came from worksheets all the students had completed. Contrary to Bob's expectations, many of his students were unable to do the problems he chose. It appeared that, indeed, many of Bob's students were not learning.

If you were Bob, what would you do? Do you think that Bob, knowingly or not, was using a teacher-as-executive approach here? Did his approach cause the problem and/or did it help him diagnose the problem? Why do you think research showed one thing about individualization and Bob found another? Was Bob really teaching?

How Much Control Is Too Much?

Elsie Simmons, a new teacher, was having second thoughts about the way she was teaching her junior literature class. At the start of the school year, her principal and colleagues had told her that the students she was getting were a rambunctious group—bright and eager, but in need of firm control. This, plus the fact that Elsie was a beginning teacher, had prompted the advice that Elsie exercise decisive control over the group from day one. Otherwise, they would take advantage of Elsie's inexperience. Research has shown that this technique produces the desired results.

Elsie took their suggestion to heart. She prepared meticulous lesson plans so that the class periods would always be under her control. And she stuck to these. The students were given specific readings to do and lists of questions to answer. During class, Elsie saw to it that she was always in charge, either through lecturing or through directing questions to students.

As she looked back on things, Elsie saw that her teaching had been successful in one respect—the students were not behavior problems. The trouble was that they were too passive. They did not seem to "get into" the material. Elsie saw none of the enthusiasm and creative energy that this group was noted for and that they demonstrated in their other classes. At best, the class's work was adequate. In addition, Elsie was upset that many of the students seemed to resent her.

Elsie had hoped to make the literature course one in which students could exchange ideas and express themselves. It did not seem to be working that way. Although she knew she would like to alter things, Elsie was not sure how or whether this could be done at this point. What should she do?

How might this teacher modify her approach? What are the pluses and minuses of an executive approach? Is this approach inappropriate for Elsie, or is it the way Elsie had implemented it that is at fault? Was this form of the executive approach a necessary first tactic?

Workbook Dilemma

Julie Karajian is a kindergarten teacher. She is considered one of the best teachers at P.S. 21, and in fact has been the subject of a documentary for network television and several articles on teacher excellence in various publications. Her philosophy of teaching is that children learn from experimentation and exploration. From this approach, Julie believes, children derive knowledge from relevant experiences and also develop an essential self-confidence needed to master future skills. Julie adapts each year's curriculum according to the type of class that enters in September. Activities reflect the group's unique learning styles. Julie is not a firm believer in the use of workbooks and learning kits, unless they are directly relevant to the children's abilities and backgrounds, which Julie has found they usually are not.

Mr. Jackson is the principal of P.S. 21. He is more interested in controlling the students in his school than anything else. He does not see children as unique individuals with specific styles of learning. Rather, he believes that most children fit into two categories: bright and not bright. He thinks teachers need to mold the children to a particular methodology, rather than vice versa. He is aware of the diverse cultures from which his students come, but he believes that in order to survive in the real world, children in this school must learn to get along as adaptive adults. He is also confident that workbooks and learning kits serve two significant functions in his school: to control students by keeping them busy and to serve as guidelines for what gets taught.

Recently, however, he has been approached by Julie concerning her class's new workbooks. She believes that because of their age level, developmental stage, and cultural backgrounds, these children will find the workbooks stifling and irrelevant. Instead of using them for a total of two hours a week as required, Julie proposes not to use them at all. Mr. Jackson recognizes Julie as the best in the school, but he firmly believes that these children need to become familiar with workbook usage and that use of the workbooks will teach them skills necessary for success in first grade. At the same time, he knows that children who come out of Julie's class often do the best in the first grade, so maybe they do not need the books as much. Besides, he has heard that Julie is tired of battling the administration and is thinking of moving to a private school. If she does, P.S. 21 will lose its greatest asset. But if the other kindergarten teachers find out that she is not using her workbooks, they will undoubtedly be angered that they are required to do so. Furthermore, what if Julie's children do not learn the necessary skills because they are unfamiliar with workbooks?

What should Mr. Jackson do? Is there some sort of compromise that could be reached? What should Julie do, as the teacher who knows her children best and who is confident about her approach to teaching? Should the teacher or the administrator be the executive?

A New Science Kit

It was the first teacher preparation day of the new school year, and Emma Dill was in her fifth-grade classroom unpacking the new materials that had arrived for her during the summer. After finding places for the paper clips, thumbtacks, and new construction paper, Emma turned to the gem of her shipment, a new science kit.

The district curriculum director, in consultation with a committee of principals and teachers, had decided on the new science curriculum to replace the textbook series that previously had been used throughout the district. Emma had served on the committee and had enthusiastically supported the choice.

Emma was one of those teachers who enjoyed teaching science. She never considered it a "filler" to finish out the last twenty or so minutes of the day. She always allotted plenty of time for science. She scheduled as many experiments as possible.

The main selling point of the new kit was that it involved experiments almost exclusively. Furthermore, all the materials except for a few common consumables were included in the kit, no small consideration in light of the time and energy Emma had spent collecting the things needed for experiments suggested by the old science text or developed by Emma herself. Even further, Emma had noted to herself with a certain amount of glee, all those teachers who had refused to do the experiments Emma considered so vital to the study of science would no longer have a way to avoid doing them.

Unfortunately (fortunately?), however, Emma had taken a summer workshop on school and society and had learned of neo-Marxist criticisms of schools. Neo-Marxists argued that the schools reproduced working-class mindsets in the children, and at the time she wondered if that really could be true. As she looked through the science kit now, she felt her enthusiasm for it wane. The kit consisted of several units. Each unit was composed of a series of activity cards stating the purpose, materials, procedure, and questions for each activity. There were five copies of each activity card, so that several small groups of students could all work at once, moving in order through each step. There was a basic serial organization of the activities and units, and it was essential to do all activities in one unit before moving to the next. Students were to be rewarded in terms of the number of units completed. Emma reflected that these features, which last spring had appeared to her to offer opportunities for experimentation, pupil involvement, and pupil self-direction, now appeared different. She wondered whether the sources of the virtue of the kits—organization and self-sufficiency—represented hidden liabilities. The kit stressed pupils' following directions over personal interaction with the teacher, prescribed goals over goals developed by the teacher and the class, following a recipe over developing a method, and so on. In short, Emma was troubled by the thought that rather than giving her students an exciting encounter with science, she was really instilling technobureaucratic values, just as the neo-Marxist theorists warned.

Do you think Emma has accurately assessed the situation? Are her fears justified? Should she use the kit? Do curriculum materials based on an executive approach to teaching reflect a technological mindset and limit teacher creativity?

Individual and Societal Needs

A: Think about it; each of us has only one life to live. Education should help each person make his or her life meaningful and fulfilling. You can't do that by forcing students to learn what they don't find personally meaningful just because it happens to be in the curriculum guide.

B: What would you teach them, then?

A: It's not *what* you teach that's really important. Don't you see? It is helping children and adolescents become themselves. Too many students just pass through the system and get treated in a mechanical way as we sort and train them for meaningless jobs and empty lives in our materialistic society. We should help them become their own unique selves.

B: That sounds good, but did you ever try to run an office or a factory full of "own unique selves"? There's nothing wrong with being your self on your own time, but when it comes to being a productive member of society, that takes cooperation and subordination of personal concerns for the greater good of all.

A: In the long run, the greater good of all depends on achieving the greater good for each individual, and that is becoming a well-adjusted, self-accepting, emotionally stable person. If our educational system could do that, nothing else would be needed.

B: What about reading, writing, and arithmetic? And what about producing doctors, lawyers, teachers, and all the educated persons required for our high-tech workforce? Be realistic, life is not always just being yourself. Each of us has to be something society needs. Schools are society's instruments for providing primarily for society's needs and only secondarily for the needs of individuals.

What do you think? What is the first obligation of the schools and their teachers, to the individual or to society? Are the views of A and B necessarily incompatible? Can both societal and individual needs be met at the same time, or is some subordination of one to the other always necessary?

Curing Shyness

Jill Yablonski was concerned about Tom, a student in her fourth-grade class. Tom was one of those shy children who always seemed to be on the fringe of things. At recess, he usually played by himself. In class, he preferred to sit quietly and listen. He did not initiate exchanges with other students or with Jill. It was not that Tom was sullen. In fact, he was a pleasant child; it was just that he liked to keep to himself. His schoolwork was good. The other children did not dislike him particularly, although they rarely associated with him. In short, Tom did not seem to be suffering from his shyness. His previous teachers all said that Tom had always been shy but had done well for them. But Jill was not satisfied with this. She thought Tom had just been ignored. Jill thought she ought to do something to help Tom learn to interact with other people.

She set about getting Tom involved. She got other children to play with him. She had Tom lead class discussions. Tom acquiesced in these activities without comment, and he seemed to handle them pretty well. Jill hoped this meant Tom was making progress.

Thus she was rather surprised when she received a note from Tom's parents, who said that Tom had become very unhappy about school. Where before Tom had always been eager to tell his day's experiences, lately he came close to tears and was unwilling to talk when asked about school. Tom's parents asked whether Jill had any idea what the problem was.

Jill did have an idea. She suspected that her program of personal growth and socialization was at the root of the matter. She was disturbed that Tom was unhappy; he had seemed to do well. She was not at all sure she should desist, though. It might be difficult in the short term, but considered in a larger perspective, Tom ought to get over his shyness. It would be a handicap later. On the other hand, maybe she was pushing things. Maybe Tom would grow out of it on his own. Maybe he was simply a shy person.

What should Jill do? Should she change her approach? Is she correct in her diagnosis of Tom? Does taking a facilitator approach to teaching mean leading a child to a goal perceived by the teacher as growth? Or does it mean permitting the child to grow in his own way? Does Jill have the right to make Tom unhappy for "his own good"? When, if ever, is intrusion in the personal development of others justified?

What Standard Shall We Use?

The faculty of Craigsdale High School is in an uproar. Susan Salerno, a new member of the faculty, has been raising questions at faculty meetings that strike at many long-held assumptions about the aims and policies of education. It all revolves around her grading policy. Susan believes that it is not fair to use a single standard of evaluation to grade all students in a class regardless of ability or level at which they begin. Such a system, she says, is not pedagogically tenable. Education aims at the growth of persons and must necessarily start at whatever level the student is at and reflect what that person is capable of achieving. A single standard against which all are graded is an externally imposed criterion that cannot measure personal growth. Further, such a standard distinguishes those who succeed from those who fail by creating failure even when a student may be doing his or her best. This system is especially untenable now that classes at Craigsdale are increasingly heterogeneous but cannot be justified even if that were not the case.

Early in the term, Susan asked her students to do a project. After giving them a grade for it and copious comments and suggestions for improvements, she had them redo the project for the end of the term. Students were then graded on how much they had improved from their first project. A student going from failing work to a *C* may get an *A* for the course. This procedure, Susan believes, more fairly evaluates student achievement and more adequately reflects what they have *learned*.

Susan's colleagues are not convinced. One of them, Tom Abelson, argues that education has traditionally been involved with setting standards of excellence for students to aspire to. Such standards are public measures of competence, and all students should be accountable to them. Ellen Myers adds that schools are expected to grade according to such a uniform standard. A system like Susan's throws into doubt the value of students' grades when they compete for scholarships or apply to schools of higher learning.

Susan replies to Tom that she is using a standard of excellence to assess student achievement. She evaluates their projects according to rigorous standards of excellence. However, when it comes to evaluating the *progress* students have made over the semester, she believes that they can only be their own measure of achievement.

To Ellen, Susan responds that it is unfortunate that the educational system is organized to a large extent the way she describes. However, that is no reason for continuing to use a policy that is pedagogically unjustified— in essence, having students compete according to a standard that may be inappropriate for them. Education should be about each person growing according to his or her own needs and abilities. Besides, grades often reflect the evaluation systems of individual teachers and are not comparable from school to school.

The case is not closed. What would you add to the continuing dialogue at Craigsdale? (Role-playing might be useful here.) Does Susan have a point about the personal-progress aspect of education? Is it fair or educative to evaluate students using a uniform standard of achievement? By contrast, can we ignore public measures of educational success or failure? Should there be standards by which all are graded? What do you think?

Teaching "Relevant" Literature

Today had been a big day for Jennifer Calhoun. For the first time as a student teacher she had taken over the junior literature classes in which she had been observing. Jennifer had put a great deal of thought into the unit on twentieth-century American literature she was to teach for the coming six weeks. The progressive theorists she had been reading about in her foundation course at State College greatly influenced her thinking, so she aimed to make the students themselves the center of her unit. She was not so concerned that the students learn to analyze literature; she wanted them to be excited by their work, enjoy their readings, and take away something meaningful from the class. In Jennifer's opinion, these things had not happened in the class up to that point.

So Jennifer spent a great deal of time developing a reading list that would be appealing and relevant to the students. She chose stories, poems, and books about teenagers, and some were even written by young people. Because the student population was diverse, she chose works by authors of different ethnic and racial backgrounds, too. The activities she developed concentrated on free discussion and creative writing assignments. She really wanted the students to become engaged with literature in a way that would help them to see themselves and to develop as persons; she structured her curriculum accordingly.

Armed with her enthusiasm and thoughtfully developed plan for meeting her goals, Jennifer introduced her unit to the classes (and to her supervisor, who was observing that day). But against her expectations, the students did not seem to be particularly excited by the readings and activities that Jennifer presented. Some even objected to them.

That afternoon, when discussing the day with her supervisor, Jennifer frankly admitted that she was puzzled and dejected by the students' reactions to her unit. The advice her supervisor offered puzzled Jennifer even more.

Her supervisor told her that by this time students were pretty set in their ways and new approaches were perceived as threatening. Also, in this junior class, many students were looking to apply to colleges. They knew that PSATs, SATs, and achievement tests were right around the corner and that standard questions on the literature sections would not be about the books on Jennifer's list. The supervisor advised Jennifer to return to the standard curriculum and standard assignments and tests. It was only fair to her students not to change things.

What would you do if you were Jennifer? Can and should the system and situational realities restrict the degree of freedom a teacher has in choosing an approach? What do you think?

Teacher and Mother?

Susie Simon was a new fifth-grader in Westville Elementary School. Eight months before, Susie's mother had been killed in a traffic accident. Susie's father was concerned that Susie needed the attention of female adults. Susie missed her mother very much, and Mr. Simon felt that he was unable to fill the roles of both father and mother. For that reason, when he enrolled Susie in Westville, he asked that she be placed in Michelle Saint Martin's class rather than in that of Mike Walsh, the other fifth-grade teacher. The principal assented to the request.

When Michelle met with her principal, he explained Mr. Simon's request. Susie needed a female role model, he said. She needed a woman to talk to and to listen to her problems. She needed affection.

Michelle listened with sympathy, but she was uneasy. She was not sure she could, or should, take on this responsibility. She had thirty-one other students in her class. Her time and energy were already extended to the limit. She could not see how she would be able to give Susie the individual attention she needed. Besides, Michelle just was not a "huggy" sort of person. Other teachers felt comfortable with overtly showing affection but not Michelle. That was not her temperament. Anyway, she did not believe such relationships were in a student's best interests. Sure, her colleagues chided her for being too straitlaced, but none doubted her skill and commitment to teaching. Weren't those the important things, after all?

Michelle wished she could help Susie. But she was not sure the principal's way was the right way. She could be a good teacher for Susie, but she could not replace her mother. Michelle had the feeling that trying to force herself to be somebody she wasn't would be hypocritical and might lead to resentment. She did not want to do anything to harm Susie. What should she do?

Is parenting a proper component of teaching? Is the principal putting unreasonable demands on Michelle by asking her to change her approach in this case? Should she try to show more affection in her teaching? Are there ways to show it without making undue emotional or physical demands? What can be done to serve the best interests of Susie and the other students? What would you do if you were in Michelle's place?

Freedom and Indoctrination

A: We all grow up in the narrow world of our parents and friends, a small place where their views, beliefs, and values become ours through the process sociologists call primary socialization. Education gives us the opportunity to free ourselves from the accident of our birth in a particular time, place, and family. It broadens our horizons and helps us to become members of the family of humankind.

B: But there are many families of humankind. There are different nations and different cultures, and that means education can't help but be indoctrination into one's national or cultural frame of mind. You may escape the narrow confines of the family you are born into through schooling, but you just trade that in for a narrow nationalistic or cultural bias. No mind can really be free. Education is a form of indoctrination.

A: Indoctrination means being taught things as if they were unquestionably true. In America, we teach people that it's all right to question, to challenge authority on logical, moral, or other reasonable grounds. Freedom is not only being allowed to do that; in a democracy it is also learning the skills needed to do it well. Learning to be a critical thinker is what a liberal education should be about. Then we ourselves can determine truth and falsity, good and evil, and not behave like unthinking sheep in a herd.

B: But a critical thinker can challenge everything and anything, right? Then even the idea of a liberal education can be challenged! And what about traditional values, beliefs, and norms? Isn't anything sacred or just plain worth not challenging because it is appreciated, it is valued, it is "our way"? Must everything be either true or false, right or wrong, when challenged by the critical thinker? Like Atlas holding up the world on his shoulders, you have to be able to stand on something.

A: That something is our belief in reason, in having good evidence for our claims, in open-mindedness, and in critical thinking.

B: But aren't those ideas just part of the Western liberal culture as it evolved over the past three hundred years? Other cultures believe in authority and tradition, in group solidarity rather than rugged individualism. Besides, even our so-called forms of knowledge are based on conceptualizations of experience that are culture laden. There's no way for a mind, initiated into the knowledge base of a culture, to be free.

What do you think? Is a liberationist approach to teaching possible? Can a person learn to overcome cultural biases? To what extent can education free the mind and to what extent must education be indoctrination?

Too Young to Be Critical?

Li Nguyen had some definite ideas about the aims of his junior high social studies class. He wanted his students to be politically aware and able to free themselves from the domination of political sloganeering. Li proposed to accomplish this through critical inquiry in the social studies. In his class, the emphasis was on giving reasons for beliefs. Unsubstantiated claims were subjected to criticism. Critical, reasoned thought was the theme of his teaching.

Li was beginning to think his class was really achieving his aim when he was called into the principal's office. The principal told Li that she had received several complaints from parents that their children had come home advocating provocative and objectionable opinions on political and social issues. This situation was unsatisfactory to the parents not only because of the content of their children's opinions but because of the way they were held. Several of the parents complained that the children would not listen to them when they gave counterarguments. The children said that Mr. Nguyen told them they had a right to their own opinions in these matters. The parents demanded immediate change. Some had gone so far as to imply that, because of his background as a political refugee, Li was not motivated by scholarship but by self-serving concerns.

The principal asked Li to meet later with her and a few of the parents in order to explain his program. Li went back to his room to consider the principal's news. He resented the implication that he was selfishly motivated. But how was he to justify his approach? He was not sure that the situation was a bad one. He felt that perhaps rebellion was a necessary first step toward critical thinking. And he believed that children *did* have a right to question accepted beliefs. However, he was disturbed that some students were unwilling to listen to their parents' arguments. He had stressed the value of an open mind. Class discussions had emphasized the need to listen to others and give good reasons for one's own beliefs. The students had seemed to learn that lesson. What should Li do? What would you say to the parents if you were Li?

Are there ages at which an emancipationist approach might be inappropriate? If so, is the problem in the manner generally, or can a valid emancipationist approach still be developed for any age group? Irrespective of age, to what extent is an emancipationist approach appropriate for teaching if it brings a community's values into question?

Education for Life

P: If we have learned anything from the past, it's that we cannot predict the future. Before the twentieth century, atom splitting was considered impossible, and no one could possibly have anticipated the problems of nuclear waste or nuclear war. Therefore, educators cannot be content to teach what we think we now know. We must prepare people for the future by teaching them how to think and how to solve problems.

T: Problem-solving is important, of course, and the future can't be known, that's true. But I believe that the best way to be prepared to face the future is with a rich knowledge of what human beings have come to know about themselves and their world and not just with some skills of critical thinking. In fact, critical thinking is best taught through a study of science, philosophy, and even art. These critical ways of thinking that are imbedded in our cultural heritage must be passed on by learning these subjects.

P: No, critical thinking and problem-solving skills are best learned, not through books and lectures on traditional subjects, but through experimentation and successful adaptations in real-life situations. Too much of schooling is a pedantic worshipping of traditions removed from the real world. No wonder students see little connection between life and what they learn in school. We must make learning meaningful, and that can only happen if people are not forced to study things disconnected from their lives but are given the opportunity to study what interests them.

T: But students are too young to know what's meaningful. We adults are better judges of what will be the rich rewards of a solid classical education. Interests can be fickle in youth. What's relevant today may not be so tomorrow. The wisdom of the past is always relevant.

P: Let's get down to brass tacks! What butcher or barber needs to know algebra or physics? What police officer, Shakespeare; or nurse, philosophy? What ordinary people need to know is how to solve *real* problems, how to be good workers, good parents, and good citizens. Your education is for an elite, not for good, ordinary people.

T: You are so shortsighted! Good, productive lives are lived by people who are enriched by their education and not just taught how to do this or that. You would give people less than they deserve in the name of practical utility. I offer them their share of their rich cultural inheritance.

How do you react to this debate? Can critical thinking and problem-solving skills be taught apart from the liberal arts and sciences? Is a traditional curriculum the best preparation for life? Does a liberationist approach require both certain subject matters and certain skills? What do you think?

Freedom of Speech?

Joan Wagner has taught American history and government at Ringwood High School for fifteen years. Her students and colleagues consider Joan to be a fair and popular teacher. In her classroom she encourages her students to voice their opinions and to keep open minds. She insists that each student receive a fair hearing from the other students. On her part, Joan feels that it is important that she not impose her opinion on her students. It would be too easy, and unfair, to push her point of view successfully, taking advantage of her popularity and position of authority. Moreover, she would not want to humiliate students who have expressed different points of view. But most important, Joan would not impose her opinion because that would run counter to her goals as a teacher—to foster students' critical capabilities and to encourage them to participate in our democratic system of government.

Tommy Jones comes to class one day with a swastika drawn on his arm and a KKK leaflet taped to his notebook. Joan does not notice at first, but her attention is drawn to these things during the course of the day because a Black boy, Steven, and a Jewish girl, Rachel, approach Tommy individually about them. Being the only Black and the only Jew in the class, they are both too self-conscious to make an issue of them. Joan decides she has to talk to Tommy.

Joan has Tommy meet her after class the next day. Tommy is still sporting his swastika and KKK leaflet and makes it abundantly clear that he knows what the swastika and the KKK represent. In fact, he has read some literature, attended a KKK meeting, and thought the matter through carefully. He has decided that White Americans must protect themselves against Jews and Blacks.

When Joan asks Tommy, please, not to come to class with such symbols, he asserts that he has freedom of speech and that he is merely expressing an informed opinion, as Joan has urged her students to do. Tommy says that he does not intend to get violent with Steven or Rachel. In response to Joan's suggestion that the beliefs of the Nazis and the KKK are offensive and threatening to Steven and Rachel even if he does not intend to hurt them physically, Tommy replies that the beliefs of Blacks and Jews are threatening to White, Christian Americans. Moreover, people have proabortion and antinuclear stickers on their notebooks. Would Joan ask those students not to come to class with those stickers because they are offensive to Tommy?

The following day, Tommy comes to class with the swastika and the leaflet in place. Joan later hears from a counselor that Steven's and Rachel's parents have suggested that they will have their children switch classes if nothing is done.

Should Joan insist that Tommy not come to class with the swastika and KKK leaflet? Should she defend Tommy's freedom of speech and suggest that Rachel's and Steven's parents likewise can exercise their freedom by switching their children's classes? Should Joan stand by while Tommy learns that he can be victorious and powerful with his swastika, since he and others might know why Steven and Rachel have left the class? Can Joan impose her opinion without countering the rules of her class, abandoning her liberationist approach, and exposing a student to humiliation? Can she raise this issue like any other issue in class, not knowing what the outcome will be as well as forcing Steven and Rachel to defend themselves? What do you think?

Mass or Class Culture?

A: Everybody complains about school being separate from life, but nobody does anything about it! Students are forced to read Shakespeare when in real life no one needs to force them to read comics and racy novels. They're forced to listen to symphonies and opera when in real life rap and country music sing to them. Art isn't in museums, but all around them in advertising and in the design of useful and beautiful products. Even our modern artists, the soup-can and comic-strip painters, saw that! Why do we persist in trying to initiate students into an artificially esoteric culture when their own real culture is so rich and satisfying? Why not help them critically engage in their culture of the real world and have school make a difference in their lives?

B: Because Shakespeare, Beethoven, and Rembrandt do make a difference in the lives of all of us. They represent some of the heights human beings have achieved, and their works speak eloquently to universal human emotions and feelings in ways barely plumbed in the pop culture. Why use mediocre examples to teach aesthetic and humane sensitivity when models of excellence are there for the taking?

A: Because students won't take them! Because students feel that their art forms are not appreciated by us. In fact, we make them feel as if their genuinely felt appreciation for their literature, art, movies, and music is a low form of uncultured, adolescent emotionalism, a phase one might have to go through but should grow out of. We treat as trivial and meaningless what they take very seriously as meaningful, as reflecting their deepest-felt emotions and needs.

B: Emotions are not what culture and art forms are about. It is intellect in its highest form that creates culture. The business of the school is developing intellect, not pampering the emotions. Television provides all the emotion, base action, and nonintellectual stimulation students need and then some. We need to counterbalance such negative cultural forces.

A: Why negative? Why must what speaks to masses of good, hardworking, plain people be negative and what speaks to only a few who see themselves as an elite be positive? Our levels of intellectual ability may differ, but all humans share the same emotional capacities to feel love, anger, empathy, caring, and joy. Our curriculum should capitalize on this capacity and use the common art forms of everyday life to bridge the gap between school and life and teach our youth about the common humanity of all human beings.

B: You win. Let's get rid of all the literature books from the storeroom and library and replace them with comics and drugstore paperbacks in our English courses. Let's clean out those old-fashioned instruments and classical records from the music room and replace them with guitars, electronic sound-enhancement paraphernalia, and the latest pop CDs. As for art, let's . . .

A: Wait a minute, we don't have to go that far, do we?

What do you think? Does popular culture have a place in the curriculum? Does teaching high culture make students feel that their culture is inferior? Is it? Is the liberationist approach elitist?

Learning Chemistry by Discussion

Mr. Tanaka's high school chemistry class had been studying how chemical elements and compounds have unique physical properties such as solubility and density. Most recently, the students had observed in experiments how compounds show characteristic melting and freezing points. When compounds were heated and the temperatures graphed in relation to time, the students discovered that plateaus occur as the compounds change physical state from solid to liquid and from liquid to gas and that these plateaus occur at different temperatures for different substances. Today, Mr. Tanaka presented a problem to his students. He explained that he had been filling a container with a colorless liquid before class and had been called away to receive a phone call. When he returned, he continued filling the container, but with a different colorless liquid that he had taken up by mistake. The container sat on his desk. Mr. Tanaka asked if anyone in the class could think of a way to separate the two liquids so that the accidental mixture would not have to be thrown out.

After good-naturedly reprimanding Mr. Tanaka for making such a careless error, the class began to think about the problem. There followed a lively discussion.

Art: That's a hard problem. I can see how one could separate marbles, say, but those are big and easy to see. Molecules are too tiny to separate.

Bernice: Maybe the liquids will separate themselves, like oil and water do.

Mr. Tanaka: Not a bad idea, Bernice. That's a technique that might work sometimes. Unfortunately, these chemicals mix completely.

Conrad: I don't know how this might work, but we've learned how molecules of different compounds behave differently. Could we use that fact somehow?

Dawn: I think Conrad is on to something there. Maybe we can't pick out molecules like marbles, but there could be some way that we could make the molecules sort themselves out.

Edgar: That's right. Like when we used filters to separate precipitates from liquids.

Mr. Tanaka: You've given some good ideas! There are filtering-like techniques, called chromatography, which can be used to separate liquids. We'll discuss that later. Can anyone think of other ways to make molecules separate themselves?

Fran: Compounds are different in how they respond to heating. Can we use that?

Mr. Tanaka: What do the rest of you think? What have we learned about heating compounds?

Grace: Well, we know that there are plateaus in the temperature-time graph where the compound changes its physical state. And different compounds have different freezing and boiling points.

Hector: I have an idea! If we heat the mixture, would one compound boil off first?

Ingrid: But how could you catch the gas that was boiled off?

Julio: What happens to the boiling points when compounds are mixed, though? Wouldn't the mixture have its own boiling point?

Mr. Tanaka: I'm pleased that you all have learned so much! Ingrid and Julio, you've raised some important problems we have to think about, but Hector is on the right track. We *can* use the difference in boiling points of some compounds to separate them when they are mixed. This isn't always easy, for there are complications, just as Ingrid and Julio have suggested. This process of separation is called *distillation*, which, coincidentally, we will study next week.

Do you agree with Mr. Tanaka that the class had learned much, even though they raised many unanswered questions? How much, if anything, has the class learned about distillation as a result of the discussion? Did the students merely learn to attach a name to a process they already knew? Or did they learn something more? How would you characterize Mr. Tanaka's manner during this lesson? Was Mr. Tanaka's teaching strategy a good one? Would it be more efficient to teach about distillation more directly? Why or why not?

Different Learning Styles

The students in Ahmad Ali's sixth-grade class seemed to fall into three groups: those who liked a great deal of teacher attention and guidance, those who worked best independently, and those who fell in between, wanting some guidance but basically self-directed.

Because of this diversity, Ahmad sometimes found it difficult to meet the needs of all his students. This problem was particularly acute for science lessons. Ahmad liked to have his students do experiments and other hands-on science activities. But equipment and materials were limited, so it was usually necessary to divide the class into small groups so that each could work through an experiment while Ahmad engaged the larger groups in other activities. This arrangement did not sit well with the independent workers, nor with those who liked Ahmad's direct guidance, however. But Ahmad justified his plan to himself on the basis of the scarcity of equipment and the need for students to learn to work together. He considered this a necessary social skill. He also believed that doing experiments was a good way to learn science. Thus he continued the small groups while taking care to be sure each contained a mixture of students with the three learning styles.

Still, he always had nagging doubts. While his students did well in science by and large, Ahmad was not sure he was being fair to the students who really preferred different arrangements. He wondered whether, if he put more thought and energy into the science lessons, he could find a way to deal better with all three learning styles and perhaps integrate different approaches into his teaching.

What would you do? What should decide one's teaching procedures and approach? Is it what students are comfortable with? What materials or equipment are available? What the teacher thinks ought to be done ideally? Is it possible to meet all students' needs? Should the teacher try to do that, or should all students learn to work together? What factors go into decisions about one's approach to teaching in a concrete situation like this?

Compatibility of Approaches

A: In their everyday teaching, teachers ordinarily use a variety of approaches depending on whom and what they are teaching. In fact, a teacher might even use a variety of approaches in the same lesson.

B: I might be able to agree with you up to a point. But we need to be careful and not overestimate the compatibility of logically different approaches to teaching. For instance, if one is a liberationist teacher, one would rarely, if ever, act as an executive who dictates the what, when, and how of learning. And a facilitator-type teacher certainly wouldn't do that either. Most teachers are quite consistent with their basic approach.

A: But you're talking as if teachers should pick one approach and stick to it no matter what, that to deviate from it would be inconsistent and unfaithful to their basic beliefs. But I'm suggesting that teachers don't need to choose one approach. They should be practical, not idealistic. Practicality calls for matching one's approach to the situation.

B: That's not practicality, that's ducking the issue. "How should I teach?" is the most fundamental professional question a teacher can ask and must answer for herself. You have to care about and believe deeply in why you're doing what you do as a teacher or else you're just acting like a robot responding with built-in external programming to the contingencies of specific situations.

A: But you need not be a robot. A teacher can really believe in the value of each approach and use each intelligently as different situations demand.

B: That sounds good in theory, but I don't think it's possible in practice. It would be like saying one can be a Christian sometimes, a Muslim sometimes, and a Jew sometimes, depending on the spiritual situation. Approaches to teaching are more like religious faiths than like hats you can put on and take off at will. They require a fundamental commitment to deeply believed views about the purpose and value of education in the lives of human beings.

A: Yes, there is that philosophical quality to the calling of teaching, but I still think a good person, a committed teacher, can believe in the use of technical proficiency in aiming both at a student's personal growth and at a depth of knowledge in the traditional subjects without being inconsistent.

B: Perhaps, but not without admitting to a failure to choose to be what one deeply believes in being as an educator.

C: I've been listening to you both and I can't believe what I hear. Choice, approach, religion, philosophy . . . ? Teaching is just a job like any other. You do the best you can, given the social, political, and local realities that you find yourself in. Whatever you might decide or commit yourself to beforehand won't make any difference once you see all the constraints of your job. All this soul searching is just wasted effort. Just learn how to do it—and do it. That's all the people want of you.

What do you think? Whose side are you on in this dispute? Why?

E Pluribus Unum

A: I've been a teacher in this school for twenty years, and I'm just amazed at how the kids have changed. We had 100 percent White, suburban kids then, and now Latinos, Blacks, Asians, even Muslims make up half the school population!

B: Well, I'm new here, and this school isn't far population-wise from where I did my practice teaching except we had many more kids from biracial marriages than I've ever seen before.

C: So what? Teaching is a color-blind profession. A kid is a kid is a kid. Kids either learn or don't. You can't tailor everything to fit each sub-population in the school.

B: But what about cultural differences? Suppose some kids learn at home that you don't talk to elders unless they address you directly first and so they don't volunteer in class. Or, some learn that cooperation and helping others (we call it copying or cheating) is how to best live your life.

C: That's not the point. We're supposed to make them American citizens, aren't we? *E Pluribus Unum!* That's our national motto. We're supposed to help them all to become believers in the same values, freedoms, and responsibilities that all citizens in a democracy have, and that means not tending to differences, but forging commonalities. You can't treat new kids differently because of their race or cultural group. That would be prejudice.

A: Yes, forming good citizens and building commonalities is important, but do you have to be "color-blind" when it's obvious that differences make a difference in how some kids learn and feel about themselves? Wouldn't it be better to be "color-conscious" so you could attend to those differences that are important to learning? We live in a pluralistic society, and it's better that we acknowledge that than act as if it isn't true.

C: OK, but then how will you ever get *unum* out of *pluribus*?

B: Wait a minute. All this sounds pretty confusing to me. I thought my job as a teacher was just to teach my subject matter. Now it seems like it's so much more. You two are veteran teachers. Maybe you could help me by describing some of the strategies you use to create *unum* from *pluribus* and when it's proper to treat some kids differently from others. And while you're at it, could you also help me understand the difference between being color-blind and color-conscious?

How would you answer B? Whose views do you identify most with? A's , B's, or C's? Why?

Go Fly a Kite

The founder and trustees of Duhey Academy have always believed that competition is an important motivator for learning, as well as a central element in the productive lives of mature persons. Many aspects of school life at Duhey reflect this basic belief. One traditional event that the students really enjoy is a yearly contest held between the sixth-grade classes to determine the best result of a class project. This year, the announced project was kite making, but for the first time in the history of the school, no winner could be determined; there was a tie! Mr. Whitehead, the headmaster, and the three seventh-grade teachers who served as judges independently rated both the class 6A and 6C kites equally on each of the points agreed upon. The class 6B kite definitely came off second best, but 6A's and 6C's entries were first-rate in all respects. So the judges declared a draw and awarded the prize, a field trip to the Museum of Manned Flight, to both classes. Mr. Whitehead wondered, though, if the educational experiences leading up to the kites produced were of equal value. Even though both products were equal, maybe the teaching/learning processes of producing them were not. He knew that Mr. Mullins in 6A was a perfectionist. He had heard that when the project was announced, Mr. Mullins had gone to the library to read everything he could about kites. Then, to the consternation of his wife, he had spent every evening in his study designing and building kites and every weekend testing his models behind the field house. When he finally developed a model that outperformed all the others, he drew up a set of blueprints and brought them to his class.

Mr. Mullins gave each student materials and a copy of the blueprint, along with careful instructions and teaching demonstrations at each step in the process. He made it clear that this was not only a contest between classes but also within 6A itself. To produce the best kite was the order of the day for each of his students. He would grade them on their effort and on their product. When they had all finished, it turned out that Jim's kite narrowly won out over Karen's, in Mr. Mullins's judgment, even though he gave each an A+. Karen's initial disappointment was softened somewhat when she found out that 6A's entry had won them a tie with 6C and a trip to the museum.

But in 6C, Ms. Goody had come at the project quite differently. As soon as she knew what the year's project was to be, she told the class and asked them how they thought they should organize their efforts to win the competition. They all knew that Robert was really good with his hands, so they asked him if he would be "quality control" helper on all the kites they produced. Others volunteered to be designers, color coordinators, supply getters, and fabricators. Before long, five small groups of kite makers formed, with each group working together to produce the best kite they could. Robert put the final touches on each and made them all ready for testing outside. The whole class witnessed the tests, and each person rated the kites on the points to be considered by the judges. Ms. Goody tallied the ratings, and 6C's entry was determined and submitted. They were all proud to learn that they had won a trip to the museum.

We haven't mentioned 6B except to say that it lost the contest. That is because Mr. Brayne didn't believe in "fads and frills." Oh, he would see to it that he met the letter of the law, and his class would have a kite for the contest, of course. Each student would be given a homework assignment to make a kite, and then he would draw a name out of the hat to see whose kite would be submitted to represent 6B. That would not take much precious class time, he figured, and so he could continue with the history unit on technology that interestingly enough treated human attempts to overcome the force of gravity through the ages. The students seemed to like the unit. It challenged their minds. Their only regret was that they wouldn't be going to the museum. They thought they would get more out of the trip than those who were going.

Do you think one of these learning experiences was better than the other? Why? What do you think was being learned in each? Imagine yourself as each of the teachers. How would you characterize what is important to do as a teacher if you were Mr. Mullins, Ms. Goody, or Mr. Brayne?

Notes

Chapter 1

1. There is a variation on the facilitator approach known as care pedagogy, which we discuss at some length in chapter 3. The philosophical and psychological base for care pedagogy is different from that used by more traditional facilitative approaches, but the ends sought by each have much in common.

2. Just as the facilitator approach contains a major variation (see note 1 above), there is also an important variation on the liberationist approach. We refer to it as emancipatory teaching, and discuss it in chapter 4. The more common name for what we call emancipatory teaching is *critical pedagogy*. We do not use that terminology in this book, for two reasons. First, we believe that *emancipatory teaching* is a more descriptive label for the character and intent of this approach to teaching, and second, we want to avoid the suggestion that other approaches to teaching are without a critical element. However, the proponents of critical pedagogy likely prefer the suggestion of Marxist and radical ideologies that typically accompany the adjectival use of *critical*. For additional information on this variation to the liberationist approach, see two of the companion volumes in this series, Walter Feinberg and Jonas F. Soltis, *School and Society*, 4th ed. (New York: Teachers College Press, 2004), and Decker F. Walker and Jonas F. Soltis, *Curriculum and Aims*, 4th ed. (New York: Teachers College Press, 2004).

Chapter 2

1. The expression *research on teaching* denotes a domain of scholarly inquiry that is well known among educational researchers. For example, the topic has generated four massive handbooks over the past thirty-five years. The most recent, the fourth edition of the *Handbook of Research on Teaching* (edited by Virginia Richardson and published by the American Educational Research Association in 2001), is 1,278 pages in length and contains 51 chapters.

2. David C. Berliner, "The Executive Functions of Teaching," *Instructor*, September 1983: 29–39.

3. Michael W. Sedlak, Christopher W. Wheeler, Diana C. Pullin, and Phillip A. Cusick, *Selling Students Short: Classroom Bargains and Academic Reform in the American High School* (New York: Teachers College Press, 1986). See also Arthur G. Powell, Eleanor Farrar, and David K. Cohen, *The Shopping Mall High School: Winners and Losers in the Educational Marketplace* (Boston: Houghton Mifflin, 1985).

4. David C. Berliner, "What's All the Fuss about Instructional Time?" in Miriam Ben-Peretz and Rainer Bromme, eds., *The Nature of Time in Schools* (New York: Teachers College Press, 1990), pp. 3–35.

5. The best description of this study for the practicing educator is Carolyn Denham and Ann Lieberman, eds., *Time to Learn* (Washington, DC: National Institute of Education, 1980).

6. The relative effectiveness of these methods and techniques and their manifestations in teaching practices are examined by Herbert J. Walberg in "Productive Teaching and Instruction: Assessing the Knowledge Base," in Hersholt C. Waxman and Herbert J. Walberg, eds., *Effective Teaching: Current Research* (Berkeley, CA: McCutchan, 1991), pp. 33–62.

7. Thomas L. Good, "Teacher Effectiveness in the Elementary School," *Journal of Teacher Education*, March-April 1979: 53.

8. B. F. Skinner, *The Technology of Teaching* (New York: Appleton-Century Crofts, 1968), p. 21.

9. Ibid., p. 64.

10. James S. Coleman, E. Campbell, C. Hobson, J. McPartland, A. Mood, and T. York, *Equality of Educational Opportunity* (Washington, DC: U.S. Government Printing Office, 1966).

11. Thomas L. Good, Bruce J. Biddle, and Jere E. Brophy, *Teachers Make a Difference* (New York: Holt, Rinehart and Winston, 1975).

12. Walter Doyle, "Classroom Tasks: The Core of Learning from Teaching," in Michael S. Knapp and Patrick M. Shields, eds., *Better Schooling for the Children of Poverty: Alternatives to Conventional Wisdom* (Berkeley, CA: McCutchan, 1991), p. 237. See also Walter Doyle, "Classroom Organization and Management," in Merlin C. Wittrock, ed., *Handbook of Research on Teaching*, 3rd ed. (New York: Macmillan, 1986), pp. 392-431.

Chapter 3

1. This description was provided by Susan Soltis in a personal letter to one of the coauthors and is used here with her permission.

2. Paul Goodman, *Growing Up Absurd* (New York: Random House, 1956).

3. Paul Goodman, *Compulsory Mis-Education* (New York: Horizon Press, 1964).

4. Paul Goodman, "Freedom and Learning: The Need for Choice," *Saturday Review*, May 18, 1968: 73.

5. Ibid.

6. Ibid.

7. A. S. Neill, *Summerhill* (New York: Hart Publishing, 1960).

8. Anne Cassebaum, "Revisiting Summerhill," *Phi Delta Kappan*, April 2003: 575-578. See also William Ayers, *On the Side of the Child: Summerhill Revisited* (New York: Teachers College Press, 2003).

9. Abraham Maslow, *Toward a Psychology of Being* (New York: Van Nostrand, 1962).

10. Carl Rogers, *Freedom to Learn* (Columbus, OH: Charles E. Merrill, 1969), p. 103.

11. Ibid., p. 125.

12. Ibid., p. 152.

13. Ibid., p. 153.

14. Jean-Paul Sartre, "Existentialism Is a Humanism," in Walter Kaufmann, ed., *Existentialism from Dostoevsky to Sartre* (Cleveland, OH: Meridian/World Publishing, 1956), pp. 290-291.

15. Carol Gilligan, *In a Different Voice: Psychological Theory and Women's Development* (Cambridge, MA: Harvard University Press, 1982); Nel Noddings, *Caring: A Feminine Approach to Ethics and Moral Education* (Berkeley: University of California Press, 1984).

16. Nel Noddings, *Starting at Home: Caring and Social Policy* (Berkeley: University of California Press, 2002), p. 17. See also Nel Noddings, *Educating Moral People: A Caring Alternative to Character Education* (New York: Teachers College Press, 2002).

17. Ibid.

18. Ibid., pp. 17-18.

19. Howard Gardner, *Frames of Mind: Multiple Intelligence Theory* (New York: Basic Books, 1983).

20. Howard Gardner, *Intelligence Reframed: Multiple Intelligences for the Twenty-First Century* (New York: Basic Books, 1999).

21. D. C. Phillips and Jonas Soltis, *Perspectives on Learning*, 4th ed. (New York: Teachers College Press, 2004).

Chapter 4

1. See note 2 for chapter 1, above, for our explanation of why we do not refer to the variation on the liberationist approach as *critical pedagogy*.

2. John Passmore, *The Philosophy of Teaching* (Cambridge, MA: Harvard University Press, 1980), p. 173.

3. Israel Scheffler, "Basic Mathematical Skills: Some Philosophical and Practical Remarks," *Teachers College Record*, 78(2), 1976: p. 206.

4. For a detailed proposal on how schools might employ this approach, see Mortimer J. Adler, *The Paideia Proposal: An Educational Manifesto* (New York: Macmillan, 1982).

5. R. S. Peters, "Aims of Education—A Conceptual Inquiry," in R. S. Peters, ed., *The Philosophy of Education* (London: Oxford University Press, 1973), p. 25.

6. P. H. Hirst, "Liberal Education and the Nature of Knowledge," in R. S. Peters, ed., *The Philosophy of Education*, pp. 87-111; also in R. F. Dearden, P. H. Hirst, and R. S. Peters, eds., *Education and Reason: Part 3 of Education and the Development of Reason* (London: Routledge & Kegan Paul, 1975), pp. 1-24.

7. Henry Giroux, Series Foreword to Barry Kanpol, *Critical Pedagogy: An Introduction*, 2nd ed. (Westport, CT: Bergin & Garvey, 1999).

8. Paulo Freire, *Pedagogy of the Oppressed* (New York: Herder & Herder, 1970). See also Freire's later work, *Pedagogy of Freedom* (Lanham, MD: Rowman & Littlefield, 1998, 2001).

9. Ibid., p. 52.

10. Ibid., p. 66.

11. See, for example, Michael Apple, *Teachers and Texts: A Political Economy of Class and Gender Relations* (New York: Routledge, Chapman & Hall, 1988); Stanley Aronowitz and Henry A. Giroux, *Education under Siege: The Conservative, Liberal, and Radical Debate over Schooling* (South Hadley, MA: Bergin & Garvey, 1985); Henry A. Giroux and Peter McLaren, eds., *Critical Pedagogy, the State, and Cultural* Struggle (Albany: State University of New York Press, 1989); Barry Kanpol, *Critical Pedagogy: An Introduction*, 2nd ed. (Westport, CT: Bergin & Garvey, 1999); Peter McClaren, *Life in Schools: An Introduction to Critical Pedagogy in the Foundations of Education*, 4th ed. (New York: Longman, 2003); and Ira Shor, *Critical Teaching and Everyday Life* (Chicago: University of Chicago Press, 1987; originally published in 1980).

12. See, for example, the following works by these writers: Patricia Hinchey, *Finding Freedom in the Classroom: A Practical Introduction to Critical Theory* (New York: Peter Lang, 1998); Ira Shor, *Freire for the Classroom: A Source Book for Liberatory Teaching* (Portsmouth, NH: Boynton/Cook, 1987); Ira Shor, *Education Is Politics: Critical Teaching across Differences, K-12* (New York: Boynton/Cook Heinemann, 1999); Joan Wink, *Critical Pedagogy: Notes from the Real World*, 2nd ed. (New York: Addison-Wesley Longman, 2000).

Chapter 5

1. Proponents of the executive approach might argue that their ends include more than subject-matter mastery, with productive employment, good citizenship, and opportunities for additional education also among executive ends. However, as one probes this position, it quickly becomes apparent that these additional ends are understood to follow from the being a good student and successfully mastering the subjects of study set forth in a standard school curriculum. In short, the additional ends are better understood as secondary ends, or as consequences presumed to follow from the primary end.

2. Jane Roland Martin, "Needed: A New Paradigm for Liberal Education," in Jonas F. Soltis, ed., *Philosophy and Education: Eightieth Yearbook of the National Society for the Study of Education* (Chicago: University of Chicago Press, 1981), p. 44.

3. Jerome S. Bruner, *The Process of Education* (New York: Vintage Books, 1963), p. 33.

Chapter 6

1. Kieran Egan, *The Educated Mind: How Cognitive Tools Shape Our Understanding* (Chicago: University of Chicago Press, 1997).

2. Ibid., p. 3.

3. Ibid., p. 23.

4. Ibid., p. 23.

Annotated Bibliography

Because we referred to a number of scholarly works directly in the main text or the notes, we reserved this bibliography for the citation of books that are more accessible and more likely to be of immediate interest to the practice of teaching. We also include a short list of periodicals likely to be of assistance to teachers; also included are a number of popular films that portray teachers.

Achinstein, Betty. *Community, Diversity, and Conflict among School Teachers: The Ties That Blind.* New York: Teacher College Press, 2002.

A study of teachers in two similar, multicultural, middle schools who seek the formation of community out of diversity but handle the inevitable conflicts that arise with diversity differently. An eye-opener showing that the climate of a school is as much or more important than the espoused mission of a school.

Ayers, William. *To Teach: The Journey of a Teacher.* 2nd ed. New York: Teachers College Press, 2001.

Ayers artfully recounts his early experiences as a teacher with rich vignettes about the children he has taught. It is a book for all teachers who care about their students no matter where they are in their careers.

Goodlad, John I. *Romances with Schools.* New York: McGraw-Hill, 2004.

Virtually all of Goodlad's dozen-plus books and hundreds of articles are within reach of the informed lay reader and all are instructive. In this latest work, he writes of his own life as an educator, and in so doing, conveys to us what is involved in fashioning a career deeply grounded in the ideals of democracy and enlightenment.

Grant, Gerald, and Christine E. Murray. *Teaching in America.* Cambridge, MA: Harvard University Press, 1999, 2002.

A sensitive and engaging portrayal of teaching, combining history, theory, and practice. An answer to the questions, What is the state of school teaching in the U.S.? How did it get that way? and What lies ahead?

Kohl, Herbert. *I Won't Learn from You.* New York: New Press (Norton), 1994.

A series of essays that turn your thinking about teaching and learning inside out. Kohl is a 1960s radical who continues to fascinate with his writings about teachers, students, and their schools.

Paley, Vivian Gussin. *White Teacher.* Cambridge, MA: Harvard University Press, 1979, 2000.

Although written a quarter century ago, this little book continues to be one of the most poignant and useful descriptions of a White teacher overseeing a classroom of children of color. A superb book for opening up discussions of diversity and multiculturalism.

Palmer, Parker J. *The Courage to Teach*. San Francisco: Jossey-Bass, 1998.
    Many teachers have gained solace and insight from this somewhat spiritual
    work on teaching. With grace and insight, Palmer presents a message of the re-
    markable potential of teaching.
Popham, James. *America's "Failing" Schools: How Parents and Teachers Can Cope with
No Child Left Behind*. New York: Routledge-Falmer, 2004.
    An informative introduction to educational accountability, standardized testing,
    and the No Child Left Behind Act. Also an important book to help you under-
    stand how testing works in American schooling and what to make of news re-
    ports about schools that are succeeding or failing.
Postman, Neil. *The End of Education* (New York: Vintage, Random House, 1995).
    A marvelous book for deepening your understanding of normativity and the
    difference it makes to education. Highly readable and informative, with an ar-
    gument sure to provoke lots of discussion.
Rose, Mike. *Possible Lives*. New York: Penguin Books, 1995.
    Even though a decade old, this affirmative portrayal of teachers and schools
    across the United States is an antidote to all the bad news one receives about
    schooling in America. Still very relevant and informative.
Tisha, as told to Robert Specht (New York: Bantam Books, 1977).
    Fascinating and uplifting story of a young teacher in Alaska during the 1920s
    and 1930s. Valuable not only because of the way it reveals the soul of a young,
    dedicated teacher, but also for its insights into the challenges a teacher faces
    when confronted with discrimination toward her students.

In addition to the books cited above, there is a great deal to be gained from the peri-
odical literature in education. Your attention is called to this limited but very informative roster of periodicals.

> *Education Next*
> *Education Week*
> *Educational Leadership*
> *Harvard Educational Review*
> *Phi Delta Kappan*
> *Teachers College Record*

Education Week is a weekly newspaper that reports education news in considerable
depth and breadth. *Harvard Educational Review* and *Teachers College Record* are two
fine scholarly journals that are directed toward a nonspecialized audience.
Education Next, *Educational Leadership*, and *Phi Delta Kappan* are monthly publications of general interest covering a broad range of educational topics. *Education
Next* often tends to have a more conservative political orientation, while the politics of the other two are somewhat less apparent. Most of these publications maintain highly informative websites, particularly *Education Week* and *Teachers College
Record*.

Popular films about teaching school are also an excellent resource. Not only are they of value for learning how school teaching is depicted in the poplar culture; they are also an enjoyable way to sharpen your skill at using the various approaches to analyze dominant teaching styles. While there are many popular films about teaching, we suggest the following for their usefulness in discussing how the teaching style of the central character is exemplary of one or more of the various approaches. All are available on VHS tape or DVD, and most can be found in local film libraries.

Conrack, Jon Voight, 1974
Dangerous Minds, Michelle Pfeiffer, 1995
Dead Poet's Society, Robin Williams, 1989
The Emperor's Club, Kevin Kline, 2002
Mr. Chips, Robert Donat, 1939
Mr. Holland's Opus, Richard Dreyfuss, 1995
Music of the Heart, Meryl Streep, 1999
The Prime of Miss Jean Brodie, Maggie Smith, 1969
To Sir with Love, Sidney Poitier, 1967
Stand and Deliver, Edward James Olmos, 1988